The Complete Book of Vegetarian Grilling

W9-AAY-663

The Complete Book of Vegetarian Grilling

OVER 150 EASY AND TASTY
RECIPES YOU CAN GRILL
INDOORS AND OUT

Susan Geiskopf-Hadler

FAIR WINDS
PRESS
GLOUCESTER, MASSACHUSETTS

Text © 2005 by Susann Geiskopf-Hadler

First published in the USA in 2005 by
Fair Winds Press
33 Commercial Street
Gloucester, MA 01930

All rights reserved. No part of this book may be reproduced or utilized,
in any form or by any means, electronic or mechanical, without prior
permission in writing from the publisher.

08 07 06 05 04 1 2 3 4 5

ISBN 1-59233-135-1

Library of Congress Cataloging-in-Publication Data available

Cover design by Mary Ann Smith
Book design by Yee Design

Printed and bound in China

Dedication

I dedicate this book to Guy Hadler, my grill-master, sous-chef, and loving husband.

Acknowledgments

I'd like to thank some of my regular diners, those taste-testers who consistently come over for dinner to prep the meal with me, set the table, and then even clean up and help load the dishwasher. Bunnie Day, Joseph Angello, Dennis Newhall, Yvonne Shanks, Candy and Al Holland, Cecelia and Michael Marsden—your help was invaluable. You all demanded that I "take a break" to enjoy a glass of wine, assuring me that you were now well fed. I also want to thank all of you not mentioned here by name for making the time to pop over for a spontaneous meal.

   I thank my husband, Guy Hadler, for letting me sleep in on Sunday mornings while he went to the farmers' market to purchase many of the fresh ingredients I used to prepare the delicious recipes in this book. Thank you also for tending to the vegetable and herb gardens as I sat in front of the computer. And your mastery of the grill is also to be commended.

Table of Contents

Introduction
A World of Delight

IF YOUR CONCEPT OF VEGETARIAN GRILLING IS LIMITED TO veggie kebabs and corn on the cob, a whole world of culinary delight awaits you within the covers of this book. Never again will you have to stand by while your meat-eating friends rave about how easy and fun it is to grill delicious meals outdoors or in. In fact, once you start serving meals from *The Complete Book of Vegetarian Grilling*, they'll be begging you for the recipes!

That's because "complete" isn't in the title by accident. From appetizers through delicious desserts hot off the grill, you'll find more than 150 phenomenal recipes for salads, light and hearty main dishes, dips, sauces, salsas, side dishes, sandwiches, and even pizza.

This book embraces the diversity of flavors and textures that can be created by cooking vegetables and fruits on the grill. The flavors, shapes, colors, and textures found in the vegetable kingdom offer endless possibilities when paired with creative seasonings, grains, breads, pastas, and cheeses. And you'll find delicious recipes from around the world to broaden your grilling horizons.

Grilling is a fast and easy cooking method that is simple to master. You can use a gas grill, a charcoal grill, or an indoor electric or stovetop grill. I prefer an outdoor gas grill for its convenience. It heats up fast, offers an even grilling temperature, ensures consistent cooking times, and is easy to clean. You can even add smoky flavor by putting wood chips on the hot grill bed. But I've included directions for every grill type in these recipes to guarantee success no matter what you're using.

Luckily for all of us who love the ease and delicious flavors of grilled food, grilling is no longer a seasonal style of cooking. Summertime is synonymous with firing up the gas or charcoal grill. The long, warm nights invite us to dine alfresco, enjoying the season to the fullest. But the cooler months are also an ideal time of the year to cook on the outdoor grill, since the heat that emanates from the grill provides warmth on a cool night. Additionally, many kitchens are now equipped with built-in grills or electric grilling appliances, turning grilling into a year-round cooking option.

Outdoor grilling is not just easy, it's entertaining. The aroma that is created by cooking on a grill in the open air excites the taste buds for the culinary pleasures to come. And of course, you're not heating up the kitchen on hot summer nights when you'd so much rather be outdoors anyway. Because grilling tends to be more casual than indoor food preparation, dining is more informal, giving you and your family or guests license to laugh and linger. So get ready to linger over the luscious array of recipes on these pages, as you plan the first of many enticing meals to come.

CHAPTER I

Grilling Tools, Terms, and Techniques

In order to be at ease with any food preparation, you have to be at ease with the tools and techniques involved. This chapter covers the essential types of grilling equipment you'll need to prepare the recipes in this book, the fundamental techniques for grilling, and basic cooking terms, along with some simple techniques for preparing ingredients.

Choosing an Outdoor Grill

A vast assortment of grills—both charcoal and gas—are available for outdoor grilling. Indoor electric grills may also be used to grill some of the recipes in this book; I'll talk about indoor electric grills on page 15. Consider how many people you usually cook for to help you decide what size grill to purchase. The biggest decision for outdoor grilling, however, is choosing between a charcoal or gas grill.

There are some pros and cons for each type. Charcoal grills traditionally burn a bit hotter than many gas grills, impart a smoke flavor, make it easier to add wood chips to the coals, and are less expensive to purchase than their gas counterparts. However, they take longer to start and heat up than gas grills, they require constant attention, they are messy because of ash and charcoal debris, and their temperatures are harder to control.

Gas grills are convenient, and the newer models get as hot as charcoal grills. Most start with the push of a button, they heat up quickly, you control the heat with the turn of a knob, and they have built-in temperature gauges. Some even come with built-in smoker boxes, or you can add a smoker box to achieve a similar effect to adding wood chips to a charcoal grill. Some gas grills also come with side burners that allow you to cook pasta or grains or to prepare a sauce while you are grilling the entrée. This feature allows you to stay at the grill, rather then go between the grill and the stovetop.

So where is the down side to gas, you ask? Gas grills are more expensive to purchase, and many grill aficionados consider "true" grilling to be cooking over charcoal or wood coals. Investigate the options, read the brochures, and talk with friends—or better yet, try out their grills!—and then decide which type of grill is right for you.

A gas grill is fueled by propane, so you have to remember to refill the propane tank or to keep a spare one on hand. If you are designing an outdoor kitchen, you can have the gas line plumbed directly to your propane line for an endless supply of fuel.

If you choose a charcoal grill, consider natural lump charcoal rather than charcoal briquettes, which contain large quantities of chemical lighter fluid. The chemicals from the lighter fluid will produce grilled foods with a harsh, acrid flavor. Lump charcoal is available in different hardwoods, such as alder, hickory, and mesquite. It starts quicker, burns hotter, and smells better than briquettes. You will need only about half as much lump charcoal as you would briquettes to achieve the desired temperature.

Some specific tools are necessary no matter what type of grill you choose; others are only necessary for a charcoal grill. Many of these tools are available only in stores that specialize in grilling supplies; others can be found wherever you shop for kitchen tools.

Tools for the Grill

These tools will make your grilling adventures easy and fun. Here's what you'll need:

- A chimney starter is a chemical-free way to ignite lump charcoal or briquettes. This large, upright, hollow, metal cylinder with a wire partition in the center will allow you to ignite coals in minutes. Look for a chimney starter capable of holding 6 quarts of charcoal.

- A disposable can or shallow aluminum tray is useful for soaking wood chips.

- A smoker box is used for placing wood chips on the gas grill.

- A long-handled, hand-held garden hoe is handy for raking hot charcoal into an even layer on the grill.

- A stiff wire brush is invaluable for cleaning the grill.

- Long-handled tongs and spatulas are perfect for turning foods on the grill and for removing the grilled food when it's done.

- Insulated mitts are essential for removing hot ingredients from the grill and for removing a hot grill rack or grill basket.

- Long-handled, natural-bristle basting brushes are handy to brush marinades on foods as they grill. Avoid nylon basting brushes because the nylon will melt when basting hot food.

- Cooking parchment or heavy-duty aluminum foil is necessary for *en papillote* cooking.

- A baking stone to place directly on the grill is necessary for cooking pizza and *en papillote* preparations. You can find them in both round and square shapes to match your grill's design.

- Cooking bricks or tiles can be positioned to hold the ends of skewers to prevent them from burning or to place foods directly on top of the grill to prevent the bottom of foods from burning.

- Large, shallow glass dishes are indispensable to hold ingredients in a single layer while they marinate.

- An assortment of metal and bamboo skewers are necessary for skewered entrées.

- A kitchen timer, or maybe two—one for out by the grill and one for inside—because you may be running back and forth between the grill and the stovetop.

- A portable flat metal grill grate or grill basket will keep small vegetables from falling through the grill grates but allow the smoke and flames to pass through the holes.

- A hinged grill basket for holding delicate foods together as you grill them is very useful. This allows you to turn the food without it falling apart because it is securely locked in place inside the grill basket.

- Cutting boards, trays, and large platters are important to place the hot grilled foods on as you transport them from the grill to the table.

Techniques for Outdoor Grilling

Grilling utilizes dry heat at high temperatures. The close contact with a hot flame quickly cooks foods and lends a characteristic grilled flavor. There is a mystique surrounding grilling, but this cooking method has been around since the discovery of fire. Become familiar with the unique features of your particular grill, stay by the grill so the food is not overcooked, and you'll soon have mastered the fun and easy skill of grilling.

There are two distinct grilling methods—grilling and indirect grilling. Grilling cooks food directly over glowing coals or the flame from a gas grill. Food is cooked at a medium to high temperature in a matter of minutes. The grill will be hooded during the cooking time except when you open it to turn the food.

Traditionally, indirect grilling calls for the fire to be on one side of the grill while the food is cooked away from the flame, on the grill but over the unlit portion. Some recipes in this book call for a slightly different indirect grilling technique where you place a baking stone or bricks on the grill to turn it into a sort of outdoor convection oven with the heat circulating around the food as it cooks. With this indirect grilling method, the food is not turned as it cooks, and the temperature is a bit lower. The grill is kept covered during the recommended cooking time.

Preheating the Grill

Grill temperatures and cooking times are not as exact as when baking something in an oven. It is important, however, to preheat a charcoal or gas grill to the temperature range called for in a specific recipe.

To preheat a charcoal grill, use a chimney starter. Place a crumpled sheet of newspaper in the bottom of the chimney starter. Place the starter on the bottom grate of your grill. Place the lump charcoal (or briquettes) in the top of the starter, filling to the top. Light the newspaper. You will see a thick column of smoke as the paper burns and the charcoal begins to ignite. Allow the coals to become orange-red in color—this will take about 15 to 25 minutes. Wearing grill mitts, dump the coals from the chimney starter into the bottom of the grill. Use a garden hoe to rake the coals into a single layer. Place the grilling grate on the grill. The coals will turn mostly to ash after about an hour. You can replenish them by raking the coals into a pile and placing unlit lump charcoal (or briquettes) on them. Leave the grill uncovered until the fresh charcoal lights.

To preheat a charcoal grill to high, light the coals and rake them over the bottom of the grill surface with the top and bottom vents wide open. Allow about 30 minutes to bring the coals to the correct temperature. This will give you a hot grill, about 500°F (260°C). You can test this by holding your hand over the coals. If you can only keep it there for about 2 seconds, the grill is hot enough. You could also use a thermometer to measure the temperature.

To preheat the coals to medium-high, follow the same procedure as described above, but rake the coals a bit thinner and allow them to burn for 5 to 10 minutes longer. You should be able to hold your hand over them for about 3 to 4 seconds, or use a thermometer to measure the temperature to read about 400°F (205°C).

A medium grill is just a bit cooler than a medium-high grill, so allow the coals to burn a bit longer. You should be able to hold your hand over them for about 5 to 6 seconds, or use a thermometer to measure the temperature to read about 350°F (175°C).

A medium-low grill is about 325°F (165°), and a low grill temperature is about 300°F (150°C). You will be able to hold your hand over the coals for about 8 to 10 seconds for a medium-low temperature or 10 to 12 seconds for a low temperature. Again, use a thermometer to check the temperature if you wish.

To preheat a gas grill to high, ignite the starter button on the grill and set the control knobs to high. This will bring the temperature to 500° to 550°F (260° to 290°C). The grill will take about 10 minutes to heat up.

To preheat a gas grill to medium-high, preheat the grill to high, and then turn the burners down to about 400°F (205°C). Oddly enough, this will take about 15 minutes because you will need to allow the grill to cool a bit.

For a medium grill, preheat the grill to high, and then back the temperature off to about 350°F (175°C). Allow about 18 to 20 minutes to reach the desired temperature. Medium-low, about 325°F (165°C), and low, about 300°F (150°C), will take a few more minutes to back off the higher initial temperature.

Best Grilling Techniques

Some special tips apply, regardless of what type of grill you use or the grill temperature you need. As with most tips, they are logical, but they are sometimes overlooked. Make sure *you* don't overlook them if you want to grill like a pro and enjoy the best, most flavorful food!

- Keep the grill clean. Fresh food will stick to leftover food that is on the grill from the last meal. Brush the grill grate after you have preheated the grill and after you have finished cooking. Use the edge of a metal spatula to scrape off large bits of food, and then thoroughly brush with a wire brush.
- Have everything you need prepped and ready at grill side before you start grilling.
- Make sure your grill tools are clean and beside the grill.
- Make sure the grill is sitting level and is stable.
- Grill in a well-ventilated, open area.
- Do not wear flowing or loose clothing. It is more likely to catch fire than snug-fitting attire.
- Preheat the grill to the correct temperature. Make sure you have enough charcoal or propane so you don't run out in the middle of grilling.
- Oil the grate just before placing food on top of it. Spray the grate or rub it with a paper towel that has been soaked with oil.

- Keep a spray bottle of water near the grill to put out minor flare-ups. Use water sparingly, as it can warp the grill and the flavor bars of a gas grill.

- Some foods will require basting as they cook. Keep your marinade and basting brush by the grill, ready to use as needed.

- Never place hot or warm coals from the grill in a garbage can! Allow coals to cool completely before disposing of them.

- Always turn off the gas grill when grilling is completed. It's a good idea to turn the propane valve to the off position on the propane tank because many grill systems will let small amounts of propane leak out, which will drain the tank prematurely.

Indoor Grills

Indoor electric grills are in their own category of grilling equipment. They offer the quick preparation that grilling on a charcoal or gas grill does, but with the convenience of indoor cooking. For those who live in cold-winter areas, and for everyone who'd enjoy grilling no matter what the weather outside, this can be a real plus. Electric grills function like inverted broilers, giving food grill marks as it cooks on the hot grate. Electric grills are not replacements for their outdoor counterparts, but they do offer a year-round solution for quick and healthy grilled meals. They are also convenient for apartment dwellers and college students. Most recipes that are cooked directly on the grill can be prepared on an indoor electric grill with slightly different, but delicious, results.

There are different styles of portable indoor electric grills available, in addition to the models that come built in on some high-end stovetop ranges. The most common are two-sided grills, combination grills, and stovetop grill pans.

Two-sided grills have two grilling plates that are hinged. They open and close like a book so that they simultaneously contact the food on two opposite sides. They are well suited to cooking sliced vegetables and some of the burger recipes in this book. The food cooks fast because the heat source cooks on both sides simultaneously. These grills usually do not have a temperature control setting, so food cooks on only one heat setting, usually medium-high.

Combination grills are shallow, 1- to 2-inch-deep electric fry pans with evenly spaced grilling ridges. The pan heats up and the food "grills" it on the grilling ridges. These grill pans come in a round or rectangular shape with a lid. You can use them at the table or on a side bar to captivate your guests as you prepare the meal.

Another popular indoor grilling method is to use a grill pan that is placed atop your gas stovetop burners. You can control the temperature by adjusting the stovetop knobs. Purchase a thick, heavy pan made of cast iron.

Techniques for Indoor Grilling

Some special tips apply to indoor grilling.

- Turn on the kitchen exhaust fan or set the grill up in a well-ventilated location.

- Oil the grill before placing food on top of it. Spray the grill surface or rub it with a paper towel that has been soaked with oil.

- Always turn off or unplug the grill when grilling is completed.

- Clean the grill between each use with warm soapy water, or, if the grill surface is dishwasher-safe, place it in the dishwasher after each use.

Basic Cooking Terms

Recipes are full of terminology, some of which can sound like a foreign language if you are not familiar with their meanings. I've listed the basic cooking terms that are used in this book here in alphabetical order for quick reference.

- **Al dente.** Italian phrase (literally meaning "to the tooth") describing pasta that is tender but still a bit chewy.

- **Blanch.** To cook briefly in boiling water; frequently done to loosen the skin of a fruit or vegetable for easy peeling.

- **Blend.** To mix two or more ingredients until thoroughly combined.

- **Boil.** To cook in rapidly bubbling liquid.

- **Chiffonade.** French technique in which leafy herbs or other greens are stacked and rolled into a loose cylinder, then sliced crosswise into paper-thin shreds using a sharp knife.

- **Chill.** To place in the refrigerator for a designated time.

- **Chop, finely.** To cut into pieces about the size of a pea.

- **Chop, coarsely.** To cut into larger, irregular pieces.

- **Cool.** To remove from the heat and let stand at room temperature.

- **Dice.** To cut into cubes of roughly uniform size.

- **Dice, finely.** To cut into very small cubes of roughly uniform size.

- **Emulsified.** Referring to a combination of ingredients that has been vigorously whipped together, often using a wire whisk, until they are completely blended and slightly thickened.

- **En papillote.** Literally meaning "in paper," a French cooking method in which ingredients are baked in a tightly closed paper packet, producing a moist and aromatic dish. *The "Pizza and en Papillote Entrées" chapter beginning on page 102 gives detailed instructions for packaging en Papillote entrées.*

- **Fork-tender.** Referring to vegetables that are easily pierced with a fork, but still firm enough to retain their shape.

- **Marinate.** To place food in seasoned liquid for a period of time, infusing it with the flavors of the marinade.

- **Mince.** To cut into tiny uniform pieces.

- **Mix.** To stir ingredients together until evenly distributed.

- **Pack, firmly.** To place an ingredient in a measuring cup or spoon and compress with your hand or a wooden spoon.
- **Pack, lightly.** To place an ingredient in a measuring cup or spoon without compressing.
- **Sauté.** To lightly brown ingredients in oil or other liquid.
- **Simmer.** To cook in gently bubbling liquid.
- **Steam.** To cook over boiling water in a covered pan, with the food suspended on a cooking rack above the water.

- **Stir.** To mix ingredients with a wooden spoon in a circular motion until well blended.
- **Toss.** To combine ingredients with a gentle lifting and dropping motion, using two implements.
- **Whisk.** To beat rapidly with a wire whisk to quickly and thoroughly blend liquid ingredients.

Simple Cooking Techniques

Even though this book focuses on the grill, some components of the preparation and presentation involve other kitchen skills. This section covers these skills, so you'll have all the directions you need in one place.

Blanching

Some recipes call for blanching, which cooks vegetables or fruits for a minute or two before peeling them or adding them to a recipe. Depending on the vegetable, this will loosen the skin so it can be easily peeled, or it will brighten the color of the vegetable to make it more attractive in the recipe.

To blanch, place a few quarts of water on to boil in a large stockpot. Wash the vegetables or fruits and leave them whole or prepare as called for in the recipe. Drop the vegetable or fruit in the boiling water for several minutes—individual recipes will give you the exact time—then plunge them into ice-cold water to stop the cooking.

To peel tomatoes, for instance, blanch the tomatoes, then simply slip the loose skin from the flesh and use the peeled tomato as called for in the particular recipe. For vegetables such as green beans, blanch them, then drain them and set aside until needed.

Cooking Dried Beans

Cooked dried beans are a wonderful source of protein and a key ingredient in many recipes. Canned beans are readily available, but the texture and flavor of freshly cooked beans are far superior. Time permitting, follow the simple procedure described below to cook dried beans.

Sort through the beans first to find and discard any small pebbles, dirt clods, or other foreign objects. Discard any beans that look moldy or shriveled. Rinse the beans in a colander to remove surface dirt, then transfer them to a large stockpot.

The smaller dried legumes, such as lentils and split peas, can be cooked without presoaking. Cover them with water and cook over medium heat for 30 minutes to an hour.

Larger beans, such as black beans or cannellini beans, need to be presoaked before cooking. To presoak, cover the beans with fresh water to a depth of about 4 inches. Cover the pot and allow the beans to soak at room temperature for several hours or overnight. If you are pressed for time, cover the beans with several inches of water as described above, then bring the pot to a boil over high heat. Immediately turn off the heat and allow the beans to sit with the pot covered for about an hour.

When you are ready to cook the beans, drain off the soaking liquid and add enough fresh water to cover the beans by about 2 inches. Bring to a boil over high heat, reduce the heat to medium, and simmer gently until the beans are tender but not mushy. The cooking time will vary depending on the type of bean, but plan on an hour or longer. Check the pot and add more water, as needed, to keep the beans fully submerged.

As a general rule of thumb, 1 cup of dried beans will yield 2 to $2^{1}/_{2}$ cups of cooked beans. You may cook beans in large batches and keep them on hand in the refrigerator for several days or freeze them in premeasured amounts for future use.

Cooking Grains

Grains are easy to cook, and they're delicious when served as a part of a grilled meal. Whole grains provide complex carbohydrates as well as vitamins, minerals, and fiber.

Different varieties of rice are called for in this book, each with slightly different cooking times that vary from 20 to 45 minutes, depending on the variety. Some rice, such as basmati, needs to be rinsed before cooking. Rice is added to rapidly boiling water, the typical ratio being 1 cup rice to 2 cups water. The pan is then tightly covered as the rice simmers over very low heat until the grain has absorbed all of the water and is plump and tender. When the rice is done, turn off the heat and set the pot aside, with the lid in place, for at least 5 minutes or up to an hour before serving.

Bulgur is a quick-cooking cracked wheat. Add it to boiling water, stir, cover the pot, and cook over very low heat for about 15 minutes. Turn off the heat and, without disturbing the lid, allow the pot to stand for 5 minutes before serving.

Measuring Ingredients

Perhaps the most fundamental technique of all is the art of measuring. Once you have spent enough time in the kitchen, you will be able to "eyeball" a tablespoon of minced cilantro or know which size lemon will yield 2 tablespoons of freshly squeezed juice. Until then, follow these guidelines. Also, keep in mind that the methods are different for measuring liquid or dry ingredients.

To measure liquid ingredients, choose clear glass measuring cups that bear red marks to delineate quantities and have a pouring spout. Place the measuring cup on a level surface, pour in the liquid, and then check the desired amount at eye level. It is useful to have several measuring cups of the same size so that you can measure and hold multiple ingredients at the same time in different measuring cups.

Dry ingredients should be measured in nested plastic or metal measuring cups that allow you to fill the cup to the brim. Dip the appropriately sized cup into the ingredient and scoop the dry ingredient into the cup until it is overflowing. Hold the cup over a plate and use a straight edge—such as the handle of a wooden spoon—to level it off.

Measuring spoons come in sets that usually range from $1/8$ teaspoon to 1 tablespoon. It is useful to have several sets of measuring spoons because many recipes will call for measures of liquid and dry ingredients. To measure a liquid ingredient, pour it directly into the measuring spoon, filling it to the brim. When measuring dry ingredients, dip the spoon into the ingredient, then level it off over a plate using a straight edge, such as the handle of a wooden spoon.

A kitchen scale is indispensable when a recipe calls for an ounce or pound weight. Sometimes you will purchase an exact quantity at the market, or in a prepackaged container, but more often you will need to measure the amount as needed. With the measuring bowl in place, use the adjusting mechanism to set the scale at precisely "o" before you place the ingredients you are weighing on it. If you are using a digital scale, follow the manufacturer's directions.

Reconstituting Dried Fruits or Vegetables

Reconstituting dried fruits or vegetables is a technique that really comes in handy. Simply place dried fruits, tomatoes, or mushrooms in a bowl and cover with hot water. Allow them to plump for 15 to 30 minutes, until they are chewable but not mushy. Remove the fruits, tomatoes, or mushrooms from the liquid and use as directed in the recipe. The soaking liquid may be reserved to use later in a soup or sauce.

Steaming Vegetables

Steamed vegetables are easy to prepare. Place a steamer tray in a large saucepan and add about 2 inches of water. Place the pan over medium-high heat and add the vegetables to the steamer tray. Cover the pan tightly and cook until fork-tender, meaning they are easily pierced with a fork but are still firm enough to hold their shape. Steaming time will vary depending on the type of vegetable.

Toasting Nuts and Seeds

Nuts and seeds add flavor and texture to different preparations, and toasting them brings out the essential oils and adds a pleasant crunch. Place the raw, unsalted nuts or seeds in a single layer in a dry cast-iron skillet over medium-high heat on the stovetop. Shake the pan as the nuts or seeds heat through. When the nuts have darkened in color to a golden brown and emit a wonderful roasted aroma, they are done. Immediately transfer them to a plate or bowl so they do not continue to cook in the hot pan. Set aside.

Ready to grill? In the chapters to come, you'll find recipes for delicious sauces and marinades, salsas and chutneys, and everything from hors d'oeuvres to desserts. Let's start cooking!

CHAPTER 2

Seasoning Sauces and Marinades

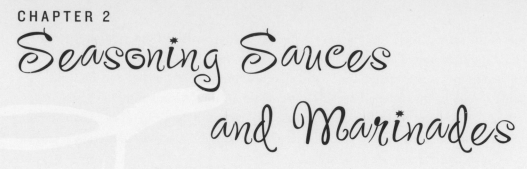

Key ingredients play a very important role in creating delicious recipes. Some of the sauces and marinades in this chapter are available in commercial preparations, but the true satisfaction— time permitting—comes from preparing them from scratch, tailoring the seasonings to your liking.

Many of the marinades are quick to prepare and can be kept in the refrigerator for several weeks until needed. Keep the Honey-Ginger Marinade (page 27), Spicy Plum Sauce Marinade (page 30), and Garlic-Soy Marinade (page 29) on hand to make almost instant tofu kebabs or to use as the base for a stir-fry dish. You can use Fresh BBQ Sauce (page 31) and Black Bean Sauce (page 32) in your own favorite recipes as well as in the ones in this book. Use the seasoning sauces and marinades as the focal point to put together that instant meal on a busy weeknight.

Some of the recipes can be prepared months ahead of time and either frozen or put up in canning jars until needed. If you grow basil during the summer and have a bumper crop, prepare batches of Basil Pesto (page 23) and freeze it in small jars to enjoy during the winter. Place a slice of fresh lemon over the sauce before securing the lid to prevent oxidation. The Tomato Coulis (page 24) is sure to become a favorite, especially if you grow pear tomatoes. I like to prepare the sauce in the late summer and put it in pint jars. I process the jars in a canning kettle and store them in the cellar to use as needed throughout the year. The sauce may also be placed in jars and frozen for several months. Make sure that you leave about $1/2$ inch of head room for expansion during the canning or freezing process.

Blueberries have a long season, and the Fresh Blueberry Sauce (page 33) is excellent over many of the grilled fruit recipes in this book. It's also delicious served over plain yogurt or vanilla ice cream. The Boysenberry Sauce (page 33) can be served over dessert or breakfast dishes, or it can be used as an ingredient to create a colorful savory sauce to serve over an entrée, such as Pistachio-Encrusted Tofu with Basmati Rice (page 143).

Basil Pesto

INGREDIENTS

2 cups (90 grams) fresh basil

1/2 cup (120 milliliters) extra-virgin olive oil

1/4 cup (35 grams) pine nuts, toasted

4 cloves garlic, chopped

1/2 cup (50 grams) finely grated Parmesan cheese

Pinch salt

Lemon slice

This is a time-tested pesto recipe. Grow basil every summer and prepare this recipe when the plants need to be snipped back. I like to prepare multiple batches, place the pesto in small jars, and freeze them to use over the winter months. Place a slice of lemon on top of the pesto—leaving about 1/2 inch of headroom for expansion—seal tightly, and freeze.

In a food processor or blender, puree the basil with 1/4 cup of the olive oil and the pine nuts and garlic. With the machine running, add the remaining olive oil in a thin stream to form a smooth paste. If the paste is too thick, add additional olive oil, a tablespoon at a time. Add the Parmesan cheese and salt and pulse to combine. Use immediately or transfer to a small jar. Place a lemon slice over the top, cover, and refrigerate or freeze until needed.

Yield: I cup (260 grams)

Mint Pesto

INGREDIENTS

2 cups (90 grams) loosely packed fresh mint leaves

1/2 cup (30 grams) loosely packed fresh flat-leaf parsley

1/2 cup (120 milliliters) extra-virgin olive oil

2 cloves garlic, chopped

I tablespoon (14 milliliters) freshly squeezed lemon juice

Pinch salt

Lemon slice

This refreshing pesto will become a favorite drizzled over grilled potatoes, vegetables, or steamed rice. It is best if used within 2 days of preparation. Mint is easy to grow. Plant it in an area where you want it to spread (and it will!) or contain it in a large pot

In a food processor or blender, puree the mint and parsley with 1/4 cup of the olive oil and the garlic. With the machine running, add the remaining olive oil and the lemon juice in a thin stream to form a smooth paste. Add the salt and pulse to combine. If the paste is too thick, add additional olive oil, a tablespoon at a time. Use immediately or transfer to a small jar. Place a lemon slice over the top, cover, and refrigerate until needed.

Yield: 2/3 cup (175 grams)

Tomato Coulis

This light and slightly chunky tomato sauce is delicious over pasta or grilled polenta. If fresh tomatoes are not in season, you may substitute one 28-ounce can pear tomatoes.

INGREDIENTS

3 pounds (1.5 kilograms) pear
tomatoes

1 tablespoon (14 milliliters)
olive oil

2 cloves garlic, minced

3 teaspoons minced fresh oregano

1/2 teaspoon salt

Put several quarts of water on to boil in a large pot on the stovetop. Place the tomatoes in a blanching basket and put the basket in the water, or simply drop the tomatoes into the boiling water. Within a minute or two, when the tomato skins begin to split and pull away from the flesh, remove the tomatoes with a slotted spoon to bowl of cold water. When the tomatoes are cool enough to handle, peel off the skins and cut out the stem ends. Cut the tomatoes in half crosswise and gently squeeze to remove the juicy seed pockets. Coarsely chop the tomatoes and place them in a bowl.

Heat the olive oil in a heavy-bottomed skillet on the stovetop. Stir and sauté the garlic for several seconds, then add the tomatoes. Cook over medium-high heat, stirring frequently, for about 5 minutes. Add the oregano and salt. Continue to cook for several minutes until almost all of the liquid has reduced, yielding a thick sauce. Set aside until needed or transfer to a jar and store in the refrigerator for several days.

Yield: 2 cups (470 ml)

Vegetable Stock

INGREDIENTS

2 medium unpeeled red potatoes,
coarsely chopped

2 medium yellow onions, diced

I red or green bell pepper, seeded
and diced

2 ribs celery, chopped

$1/2$ pound (225 grams) mushrooms, chopped

2 cups (200 grams) assorted
vegetables, chopped

6 cloves garlic, chopped

2 bay leaves

2 teaspoons dried basil

I teaspoon dried thyme

I teaspoon salt

$1/2$ teaspoon ground pepper

Any combination of vegetables, including fresh or dried mushrooms, and a variety of herbs can be included in a stock. The key is to balance the flavor because you do not want a specific vegetable to dominate. Use the stems, stalks, and outer lettuce leaves that you would otherwise throw away as part of your assorted vegetable mix. It is always good to add a potato or two to give the stock some body. You may freeze this in measured amounts to use as needed. Measurements are given here, but don't feel compelled to measure exactly.

Put 14 cups (3 liters) water in a large stockpot on the stovetop over medium-high heat. Add all the ingredients. Bring to a boil. Reduce the heat to low and simmer, uncovered, for about an hour. Turn off the heat and allow the mixture to cool for about 15 minutes before straining into a separate pot. Set aside to use immediately or transfer to a container and refrigerate for several days or freeze for several months.

Yield: about 10 cups (2.5 liters)

Soy and Balsamic
Fusion Marinade

This combination is a mix of Asian and Mediterranean ingredients that is wonderful with mushrooms and with tempeh dishes.

INGREDIENTS

$1/4$ cup (60 milliliters) dry sake

3 tablespoons (45 milliliters)
   soy sauce

I tablespoon (14 milliliters)
   dark sesame oil

I tablespoon (14 milliliters)
   balsamic vinegar

I tablespoon (14 milliliters)
   vegetarian Worcestershire sauce

I clove garlic, minced

$1/4$ teaspoon dried tarragon

Place the sake, soy sauce, sesame oil, balsamic vinegar, and Worcestershire sauce in a medium bowl and whisk together. Add the garlic and tarragon and whisk to combine. Use the sauce immediately or refrigerate until needed.

Yield: $1/2$ cup (120 milliliters)

Honey-Ginger
Marinade

Many different ingredients are delicious when marinated in this mixture. I especially like it with tofu.

INGREDIENTS

6 tablespoons (90 milliliters)
  freshly squeezed lemon juice

3 tablespoons (45 milliliters)
  dark sesame oil

3 tablespoons (45 milliliters)
  soy sauce

3 tablespoons (60 grams) honey

3 teaspoons minced fresh ginger

3 cloves garlic, minced

Prepare the marinade in a medium bowl by whisking together the lemon juice, sesame oil, soy sauce, honey, ginger, and garlic. Use the marinade immediately or refrigerate until needed.

Yield: I cup (235 milliliters)

Raspberry Vinegar Marinade

INGREDIENTS

2 tablespoons (28 milliliters)
 raspberry vinegar

1 tablespoon (14 milliliters)
 dark sesame oil

1 tablespoon (14 milliliters)
 soy sauce

3 teaspoons maple syrup

You will find many uses for this marinade, especially with winter root vegetables.

Put the raspberry vinegar, sesame oil, soy sauce, and maple syrup in a small bowl and whisk to combine. Use the marinade immediately or refrigerate until needed.

Yield: $1/3$ cup (90 milliliters)

Garlic-Soy Marinade

This combination of flavors works well with tofu or squashes.

INGREDIENTS

$^1/_2$ cup (120 milliliters) freshly
squeezed orange juice

3 tablespoons (45 milliliters)
toasted sesame oil

2 tablespoons (28 milliliters) soy
sauce

3 cloves garlic, minced

1 teaspoon dried basil, crushed

Prepare the marinade in a medium bowl by whisking together the orange juice, sesame oil, soy sauce, garlic, and basil. Use immediately as a marinade or refrigerate until needed.

Yield: $^3/_4$ cup (175 milliliters)

Spicy Plum Sauce Marinade

INGREDIENTS

1/4 cup (75 grams) plum sauce

1/4 cup (60 milliliters) freshly
squeezed lemon juice

2 tablespoons (28 milliliters)
soy sauce

I teaspoon dried red chili flakes,
crushed

Spicy and sweet, this marinade is a flavorful way to season tofu for the grill. Plum sauce, the base ingredient of this marinade, is available in Asian markets.

Place the plum sauce, lemon juice, soy sauce, and chili flakes in a small bowl and whisk to combine. Use immediately or cover and refrigerate for several days.

Yield: 1/2 cup (120 milliliters)

Fresh BBQ Sauce

INGREDIENTS

1 1/2 pounds (700 grams) pear
    tomatoes

2 tablespoons (28 milliliters)
    canola oil

1 medium yellow onion, chopped

2 tablespoons (16 grams) grated
    fresh ginger

6 teaspoons fermented black
    beans, rinsed

4 cloves garlic, minced

2 serrano chiles, seeded and
    minced

1/4 cup (60 milliliters) rice wine
    vinegar

1/4 cup (60 milliliters) soy sauce

2 tablespoons (40 grams) honey

Several grinds black pepper, to
    taste

This flavorful sauce has many uses. Try it not only with tofu, as called for in this book, but also with potatoes or on top of scrambled eggs. You may use molasses instead of honey for a flavor variation.

Place several quarts of water in a stockpot on the stovetop and bring to a boil over high heat. Place the tomatoes in a blanching basket and put the basket in the water, or simply drop the tomatoes into the boiling water. Within a minute or two, when the tomato skins begin to split and pull away from the flesh, remove the tomatoes with a slotted spoon to a bowl of cold water. When the tomatoes are cool enough to handle, peel off the skins and coarsely chop. Set aside.

Place the canola oil in a large skillet on the stovetop over medium-high heat and add the onion, ginger, fermented black beans, garlic, and serrano chiles. Cook for 8 to 10 minutes, stirring frequently. Add the tomatoes, reduce the heat to medium-low, and continue to cook for about 15 minutes. Add the rice wine vinegar, soy sauce, honey, and black pepper and cook for an additional 5 minutes. Remove from the heat and place in a food processor. Blend until smooth. Keep refrigerated until needed. This sauce will hold over in the refrigerator for about 2 weeks.

Yield: 4 cups (950 milliliters)

Black Bean Sauce

INGREDIENTS

1/2 cup (85 grams) fermented
    black beans, not rinsed

1/4 cup (60 milliliters) mirin

2 tablespoons (28 milliliters)
    soy sauce

I tablespoon (14 milliliters)
    canola oil

I tablespoon (9 grams)
    brown sugar

3 cloves garlic, minced

2 teaspoons grated fresh ginger

Pinch dried red chili flakes

Fermented black beans can be found in Asian markets, packed in jars. You will also find them in many health food stores and well-stocked supermarkets. Depending on how you are going to use this sauce, you may leave the beans whole, chop them, or puree them. You can find mirin (rice wine) where you find the fermented black beans.

Place the fermented black beans, mirin, soy sauce, canola oil, brown sugar, garlic, ginger, and chili flakes in a blender along with 3 tablespoons (45 milliliters) water. Puree until smooth. Place in a small jar and refrigerate until needed. This sauce will stay fresh in the refrigerator for about 2 weeks.

Yield: 3/4 cup (90 milliliters)

Fresh Blueberry Sauce

As a variation, you may use raspberries or blackberries for this sauce. I use Meyer lemon juice because it is slightly sweeter than other varieties. You can add more honey if the sauce is too tart. Use this sauce as the base for a reduction sauce or pour it over grilled fruit desserts.

INGREDIENTS

2 cups (290 grams) fresh blueberries

$^1/_4$ cup (85 grams) honey

1 tablespoon (14 milliliters) freshly squeezed lemon juice

$^1/_4$ teaspoon salt

$^1/_2$ teaspoon vanilla

Wash the blueberries and place them in a bowl. Use a masher or slotted spoon to crush them. Stir in the honey, lemon juice, and salt. Place the mixture in a small saucepan on the stovetop and bring to a boil over high heat. Boil for about a minute, stirring to make sure the bottom doesn't scorch. Add the vanilla. Remove the saucepan from the heat and set aside to cool.

Place a sieve over a bowl and pour the sauce into it. Mash the berries with the back of a wooden spoon to press all of the sauce into the bowl. Discard the berry pulp. Transfer the sauce to a jar and refrigerate until needed, for up to 4 weeks.

Yield: 1 cup (235 milliliters)

Boysenberry Sauce

My friends Paul and Lizz Blaise have a boysenberry patch in their yard that yields a bumper crop every year. Lizz prepares this sauce and uses it over pancakes, waffles, and French toast or to flavor yogurt and ice cream. It became the inspiration for Pistachio-Encrusted Tofu with Basmati Rice (page 143).

INGREDIENTS

7 cups (770 grams) fresh boysenberries

1 cup (200 grams) sugar

Place the boysenberries and sugar in a large pot on the stovetop over medium-high heat and bring to a boil. Reduce to a slow boil and cook, covered, for about 45 minutes. Remove the lid, reduce the heat to medium-low, and continue to cook for about 2 hours, stirring occasionally. (The berries will break up as the sauce thickens.) Remove the pot from the heat and allow to cool. Place a large sieve over a bowl and pour the sauce into it. Mash the berries with the back of a wooden spoon to press all of the sauce into the bowl. Discard the berry pulp. Transfer the sauce to a jar and refrigerate until needed, for up to 4 weeks. The sauce may also be frozen.

Yield: 2$^1/_2$ cups (970 g)

CHAPTER 3

Salsas, Chutneys, and Dipping Sauces

These simple combinations of vegetables, fruits, condiments, and spices yield the "secret sauce" component for many fantastic meals. I have recommended specific salsas, chutneys, and dipping sauces to accompany many of the recipes throughout the book, but you should feel free to experiment with mixing and matching to discover your own favorite combinations.

Some of these recipes, such as the Salsa Fresca (page 45), Creamy Horseradish Sauce (page 53), Grilled Red Bell Pepper Mayonnaise (page 47), and the Dilled Yogurt and Sour Cream Sauce (page 51) can be prepared ahead of time and kept in closed containers in the refrigerator for several days. Chutney will also hold over in the refrigerator for up to a week. Other fresh fruit combinations are best prepared right before serving. The Peach and Blueberry Salsa (page 36), Guacamole (page 48), and Mango and Papaya Salsa with Jalapeños (page 37) are best prepared when the ingredients are at the height of the season and serve at room temperature.

Choose large, shallow bowls to serve salsas or chutneys in or place several smaller shallow bowls around the table. Serve the dipping sauces in individual ramekins or very small bowls so the diners can repeatedly dip into their own serving of sauce.

Peach and Blueberry Salsa

INGREDIENTS

2 medium white peaches, peeled, seeded,
 and diced

$^1/_3$ cup (50 grams) blueberries, halved

2 green onions, minced

I tablespoon (14 milliliters) olive oil

I teaspoon balsamic vinegar

2 teaspoons lime juice

$^1/_2$ teaspoon crushed garlic

3 teaspoons minced fresh sage

6 teaspoons minced fresh basil

The delicate white peaches pair with the richly colored berries to carry the flavors of this salsa. Serve it with fajitas or skewered entrées or simply enjoy it with corn chips.

Gently combine the peaches, blueberries, and green onions in a medium bowl.

In a separate bowl, whisk together the olive oil, balsamic vinegar, lime juice, garlic, sage, and basil. Pour over the peach mixture and toss to combine. Allow the flavors to blend at room temperature for about 1 hour before serving. Use immediately or refrigerate overnight.

Yield: 4 cups (I kilogram)

Mango and Papaya
Salsa with Jalapeños

This salsa has a bit of a bite to it that is soothed by the sweetness of the fruit. Try it with Tempeh, Pineapple, and Jalapeño Skewers (page 157) or Brie and Mango Quesadillas (page 186).

INGREDIENTS

I firm, ripe mango, peeled, seeded, and diced

2 cups (280 grams) peeled, seeded, and diced papaya

I cup (145 grams) blueberries, halved

4 green onions, minced

1/4 cup (10 grams) minced fresh basil

2 tablespoons (28 milliliters) olive oil

I teaspoon balsamic vinegar

I tablespoon (14 milliliters) lime juice

2 cloves garlic, minced

2 jalapeño chiles, seeded and minced

Gently combine the mango, papaya, blueberries, green onions, and basil in a medium bowl.

In a separate bowl, whisk together the olive oil, balsamic vinegar, lime juice, garlic, and jalapeño chiles. Pour over the mango mixture and toss to combine. Allow the flavors to blend at room temperature for about 1 hour before serving. Use the salsa immediately or refrigerate overnight.

Yield: 4 cups (I kilogram)

Smooth Tomatillo Salsa

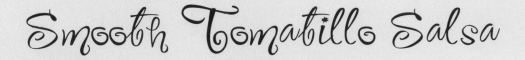

INGREDIENTS

I pound (455 grams) fresh
   tomatillos, in the husk

¹/₄ cup (40 grams) minced white
   onion

¹/₄ cup (4 grams) minced fresh
   cilantro

I tablespoon (14 milliliters) freshly
   squeezed lime juice

I jalapeño chile, seeded and
   minced

2 cloves garlic, minced

¹/₄ teaspoon salt

This salsa is smooth when first prepared, but once refrigerated it turns into a jelly-like consistency. To return it to a smooth salsa, bring it to room temperature and add a tablespoon or so of warm water. Stir to combine.

Place the tomatillos, still in their husks, in a plastic bag and fill the bag with water. Seal and allow the tomatillos to soak for about 15 minutes.

   Preheat the grill to high with a smoker box in place. Remove the tomatillos from the bag and place them on the grill. Grill for 15 to 18 minutes, turning frequently. (The husks will char slightly, but they should not totally blacken.) Remove the tomatillos from the grill and set aside to cool. When the tomatillos are cool enough to handle, remove and discard the husks and place the tomatillos in a food processor. Pulse to chop and add the onion, cilantro, lime juice, jalapeño chile, garlic, and salt. Puree until smooth. Transfer to a serving bowl.

Yield: 2 cups (500 grams)

Pear and Avocado Salsa

INGREDIENTS

1 Bartlett pear, peeled, seeded, and diced

1 medium Haas avocado, seeded, peeled, and diced*

1 large jalapeño chile, seeded and minced

3 teaspoons minced fresh cilantro

3 teaspoons minced fresh flat-leaf parsley

1 green onion, minced

1 tablespoon (14 milliliters) olive oil

1 tablespoon (14 milliliters) lime juice

$1/8$ teaspoon granulated garlic

Pinch salt

This salsa can be prepared any time of the year to enjoy as an appetizer or to serve with a skewered entrée. Have all of your other ingredients prepared and set aside before you peel and dice the pear so it doesn't turn brown. Haas avocados are the ones with pebbled dark green or black skin.

Place the pear, avocado, and jalapeño chile in a medium bowl and gently toss to combine. Add the cilantro, parsley, and green onion, tossing to combine.

In a separate bowl, whisk together the olive oil, lime juice, garlic, and salt. Pour over the pear mixture and gently toss to combine. Allow the flavors to blend at room temperature for about 1 hour before serving.

Yield: 2 cups (500 g)

* Cut the avocado in half, remove the pit, then slice the shell and spoon out the avocado.

Pear-Cantaloupe Salsa

INGREDIENTS

2 Bartlett pears, peeled, seeded, and diced

2 cups (310 grams) diced cantaloupe

2 tablespoons (28 milliliters) lemon juice

1/2 cup (45 grams) diced red bell pepper

6 teaspoons minced fresh cilantro

2 green onions, minced

1/3 cup (75 milliliters) rice vinegar

The colors in this salsa are a feast for the eyes. Prepare it in the late summer when all of the ingredients are fresh at the farmers' market. Have all of your other ingredients prepared and set aside before you peel and dice the pears so they don't turn brown.

Place the pears and cantaloupe in a medium bowl and toss with the lemon juice. Add the bell peppers, cilantro, and green onions. Toss to combine. Drizzle the rice vinegar over the pear mixture, then toss to combine. Allow the flavors to blend at room temperature for about 1 hour before serving. Use the salsa immediately or refrigerate overnight.

Yield: 4 cups (1 kilogram)

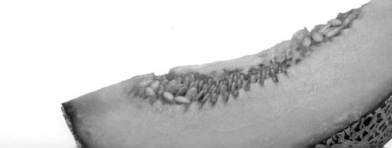

Peach and Pineapple Salsa
with Fresh Tarragon

INGREDIENTS

2 peaches, peeled, seeded, and diced

$1/2$ cup (80 grams) diced pineapple

$1/3$ cup (30 grams) diced green bell pepper

I green onion, minced

I jalapeño chile, seeded and minced

2 teaspoons sherry vinegar

I teaspoon minced fresh tarragon

The sweet peaches and the slightly acidic pineapple combine to make this salsa a spring treat. The jalapeño adds just the right heat to the sweetness—add more jalapeño if you want the salsa to be spicier. You may also want to add more tarragon, depending on the fresh variety that is available to you. Taste and see!

Place the peaches, pineapple, bell pepper, green onion, and jalapeño chile in a bowl and gently toss to combine.

In a separate bowl, whisk together the sherry vinegar and tarragon. Pour over the peach mixture and gently toss to combine. Allow the flavors to blend at room temperature for about 1 hour before serving.

Yield: 2 cups (500 g)

Jícama and Mango Salsa
with Jalapeños

INGREDIENTS

2 cups (240 grams) peeled and diced jícama

1 firm, ripe mango, peeled, seeded, and diced

2 firm, ripe kiwis, peeled and diced

1/3 cup (55 grams) diced red onion

2 jalapeño chiles, seeded and finely diced

5 teaspoons minced fresh cilantro

3 tablespoons (45 milliliters) freshly squeezed lime juice

The crisp jícama and the sweet mango, with the slightly hot jalapeños, combine to make this a sweet, slightly hot salsa. This salsa is great with chips, quesadillas, and tofu tacos. It's best used the day it's prepared.

Place the jícama, mango, kiwis, red onion, and jalapeño chiles in a medium bowl and toss to combine. Add the cilantro and lime juice, gently toss again, and set aside until needed.

Yield: 6 cups (1.5 kilograms)

Salsa Fresca

INGREDIENTS

4 Anaheim chiles

2 1/2 pounds (1.25 kilograms) pear
    tomatoes

1/4 cup (60 milliliters) freshly
    squeezed lime juice

1/2 cup (80 grams) minced white
    onion

1/4 cup (4 grams) minced fresh
    cilantro

2 cloves garlic, minced

1/8 teaspoon salt

Tomatoes, chiles, and fresh cilantro are the foundation of a great salsa. This one is simple to prepare. The recipe may be doubled or tripled if you like to put foods in canning jars and process to preserve. The quantity this recipe yields will stay fresh for about 10 days in the refrigerator.

Preheat the grill to high. Place the Anaheim chiles directly on the grill and grill for 8 to 10 minutes, turning frequently. (The skins will blacken.) Remove the chiles from the grill and place in a plastic bag. Seal the bag and set aside to cool. When the chiles are cool enough to handle, peel off the charred skin and place the chiles on a cutting board. Slice the chiles lengthwise, removing the stem ends and seeds. Chop the chiles and set aside.

Place several quarts of water in a large stockpot on the stovetop and bring to a boil over high heat. Place the tomatoes in a blanching basket and put the basket in the water, or simply drop the tomatoes into the boiling water. Within a minute or two, when the tomato skins begin to split and pull away from the flesh, remove the tomatoes with a slotted spoon to a bowl of cold water. When the tomatoes are cool enough to handle, peel off the skins and cut out the stem ends. Cut the tomatoes in half crosswise. Gently squeeze the tomatoes over the sink to remove the juicy seed pockets, then dice the tomatoes and place them in a bowl. Drain off any juice. Add the chopped chiles, lime juice, onion, cilantro, garlic, and salt. Serve immediately or refrigerate until needed.

Yield: 5 cups (1125 grams)

Peanut Sauce

INGREDIENTS

2 tablespoons (30 grams) creamy
  peanut butter

2 tablespoons (28 milliliters)
  freshly squeezed lemon juice

I tablespoon (20 grams) honey

I tablespoon (17 grams) light-
  colored miso

I tablespoon (14 milliliters) mirin
  (rice wine)

I teaspoon (14 milliliters) soy sauce

*Peanut sauce is a wonderful complement to a tofu or tempeh dish.
You will also enjoy this sauce with jícama slices, celery sticks, and baby
carrots. This sauce may be covered and refrigerated overnight, but bring
it back to room temperature before serving.*

Place the peanut butter, lemon juice, honey, miso, mirin, and soy
sauce in a medium bowl, along with $^1/_2$ cup (120 milliliters) hot
water, and whisk together until smooth. Set aside until needed.

Yield: $^3/_4$ cup (90 milliliters)

Garlic-Herb Mayonnaise

INGREDIENTS

$^3/_4$ cup (175 grams) mayonnaise

2 tablespoons (28 milliliters)
  freshly squeezed lemon juice

3 teaspoons minced fresh thyme

3 teaspoons minced fresh flat-leaf
  parsley

6 teaspoons chopped fresh chives

$^1/_2$ teaspoon crushed garlic

3 to 4 drops Tabasco-style hot
  sauce

*Try this for a fast, flavorful mayonnaise. It makes a yummy dip for
grilled veggies as well as a tasty spread for wraps and sandwiches.*

Place the mayonnaise, lemon juice, thyme, parsley, chives, garlic,
and hot sauce in a medium bowl and whisk to combine. Transfer to
a serving dish and use immediately or cover and refrigerate for up
to 2 days.

Yield: $^3/_4$ cup (175 grams)

Grilled Red Bell Pepper *Mayonnaise*

INGREDIENTS

1 red bell pepper

1 large egg yolk

1 cup (235 milliliters) extra-virgin
olive oil

2 tablespoons (28 milliliters)
freshly squeezed lemon juice

1 teaspoon crushed garlic

Pinch salt

Several grinds black pepper, to
taste

*Homemade mayonnaise elevates this common condiment to new heights.
Once mastered, you can prepare many variations to serve as sauces or
spreads. They will hold over in the refrigerator for about a week.*

Preheat the grill to high. Place the bell pepper directly on the grill
and grill for 10 to 15 minutes, turning frequently. Grill until the
skin is charred black. Transfer the pepper to a plastic or paper bag,
close the bag, and set aside for about 15 minutes.

Meanwhile, place the egg yolk in a blender and pulse briefly.
With the blender running, add the olive oil in a steady stream. (The
egg and oil will emulsify into a thick sauce.) Add the lemon juice,
garlic, salt, and black pepper and pulse to combine.

When the bell pepper is cool enough to handle, peel off the
charred skin and discard the seeds, stem, and white membrane.
Coarsely chop the pepper and add to the blender. Pulse to blend for
a few seconds to create a smooth mayonnaise. Transfer to a jar and
refrigerate for an hour or up to 1 week before serving.

Yield: 2 cups (700 g)

Guacamole

Guacamole is one of the signature dishes of Mexico, but those of us north of the border love this spicy avocado dip, too. This version is best prepared right before serving. Haas avocados are the ones with pebbled dark green or black skin.

INGREDIENTS

2 medium-ripe Haas avocados, seeded, peeled, and diced

2 tablespoons (28 milliliters) freshly squeezed lime juice

$^1/_3$ cup (55 grams) minced white onion

I clove garlic, minced

I medium jalapeño chile, seeded and minced

$^1/_4$ teaspoon ground cumin

$^1/_4$ teaspoon salt

$^1/_8$ pound (55 grams) cherry tomatoes, diced (about 6 cherry tomatoes)

Place the avocados in a bowl. Add the lime juice, onion, garlic, jalapeño chile, cumin, and salt and mash with a fork until no large chunks remain. Stir in the tomatoes. Serve immediately or set aside at room temperature for up to 1 hour.

Yield: 2 cups (450 grams)

Mexican Crema

A slightly soured cream is often served in Mexico as a table condiment. Many of the dishes in this book are delightful when served with fresh crema. This sauce is found in Mexican markets, but it can be simply prepared at home.

INGREDIENTS

I cup (235 milliliters) heavy whipping cream

I tablespoon (14 milliliters) buttermilk

Pour the cream into a small saucepan on the stovetop. Heat the cream over low heat to bring it to a lukewarm temperature. (Do not heat it to more than 100°F.) Stir in the buttermilk and transfer the mixture to a glass jar. Loosely set the lid on the jar, but do not tighten. Set the jar aside in a warm place—80° to 90°F (28° to 32°C)—for 12 to 24 hours. (The crema will culture, becoming some-what thick.) Stir with a wooden spoon, tighten the lid, and refrigerate for about 4 hours to chill before serving. (The crema will continue to thicken a bit as it chills.) Keep refrigerated and use within 2 weeks of preparation.

Yield: I cup (230 grams)

Spicy Tahini Sauce

This sauce is delicious served over a pasta dish or as a dipping sauce for grilled vegetables

INGREDIENTS

- I cup (235 milliliters) Vegetable Stock (page 25)
- 3 tablespoons (45 grams) toasted sesame tahini
- 2 tablespoons (28 milliliters) soy sauce
- I tablespoon (14 milliliters) rice vinegar
- I tablespoon (8 grams) grated fresh ginger
- I tablespoon (20 grams) honey
- $1/4$ teaspoon red chili flakes, crushed

In a saucepan, whisk together the Vegetable Stock, tahini, soy sauce, rice vinegar, ginger, honey, and chili flakes. Place on the stovetop and bring to a boil. Reduce the heat to medium-low and simmer for about 5 minutes. Set aside until needed.

Yield: I $1/4$ cups (300 grams)

Dilled Yogurt
and Sour Cream Sauce

INGREDIENTS

1/2 cup (125 grams) low-fat plain yogurt

1/2 cup (115 grams) low-fat sour cream

1 tablespoon (14 milliliters) red wine
vinegar

1 teaspoon dried dill weed, crushed

1/2 teaspoon crushed garlic

1/8 teaspoon salt

Several grinds black pepper, to taste

This sauce is very easy to prepare, and it is best made ahead of time so the flavors can blend. It is good with grilled potatoes, vegetables, and tofu entrées.

Place the yogurt and sour cream in a small bowl and whisk in the red wine vinegar, dill, garlic, salt, and black pepper. When well combined, cover and refrigerate until needed. Uncover and serve or transfer to individual dipping bowls.

Yield: 1 cup (235 milliliters)

Creamy Ponzu Sauce

INGREDIENTS

1/4 cup (60 milliliters) ponzu sauce

1/8 cup (30 grams) sour cream

1 tablespoon (14 milliliters) freshly
squeezed lime juice

Ponzu sauce is a citrus-seasoned soy sauce that you will find at some supermarkets or any Asian market. Once you've bought the basic ponzu sauce, this is a very fast and easy sauce to prepare. Keep the ingredients on hand to whip this up to complement many grilled dishes.

In a small bowl, whisk together the ponzu sauce, sour cream, and lime juice. Serve immediately or refrigerate until needed.

Yield: 3/4 cup (90 milliliters)

Remoulade Sauce

This classic French sauce is easy to prepare and delicious with grilled vegetables or as a spread on sandwiches.

INGREDIENTS

1 cup (235 grams) mayonnaise

1 tablespoon (15 grams) Dijon mustard

2 tablespoons (30 grams) sweet pickle relish

2 tablespoons (15 grams) minced capers

3 teaspoons minced fresh tarragon

Place the mayonnaise in a small bowl and add the mustard, relish, capers, and tarragon. Stir until well combined. Place in a small jar and refrigerate until needed.

Yield: 1 1/8 cups (300 grams)

Creamy Horseradish Sauce

This sauce is wonderful with grilled potatoes, eggplant, tofu, or tempeh.

INGREDIENTS

1 cup (230 grams) sour cream

1 tablespoon (15 grams) ketchup

1 tablespoon (14 milliliters) freshly squeezed lemon juice

1 teaspoon vegetarian Worcestershire sauce

2 teaspoons prepared horseradish

Pinch salt

Several grinds black pepper, to taste

Place the sour cream in a bowl and whisk in the ketchup, lemon juice, Worcestershire sauce, horseradish, salt, and black pepper. Set aside in the refrigerator for 1 hour or up to overnight so the flavors can blend.

Yield: 1 1/4 cups (300 milliliters)

CHAPTER 4

Hors d'Oeuvres, Dips, and Spreads

Hors d'oeuvres—French for appetizers, the food served at the beginning of the meal—go way beyond cheese and crackers or salsa and chips. Adding the grill as a cooking method opens the door to interesting appetizers, innovative dips, and savory spreads. They can be casual or fancy in their presentation, eaten with fingers or a fork, and enjoyed standing up or sitting down. Serve a single hors d'oeuvre to begin a meal or serve several together for a fun cocktail party.

Most of these grilled hors d'oeuvres are simple to prepare. The recipes can be doubled to feed a crowd, and they can be made ahead of time, before your guests arrive, so you can spend more time enjoying the festivities. Mushrooms Stuffed with Couscous, Mint Pesto, and Walnuts (page 62), Crostini with Grilled Zucchini and Eggplant (page 66), and Grilled Spinach Rolls Stuffed with Tofu and Feta (page 58) make a tasty finger-food buffet.

Get creative with the presentation by using pretty plates and bowls, edible flowers and herbs, and a colorful array of napkins. Set the hors d'oeuvres out where you want your guests to gather and serve your favorite libations. Mingle with the crowd to enjoy the lively conversations. Prepare and stage the Purple Figs Stuffed with Blue Cheese (page 57) in advance, and then grill with your guests present for a bevy of comments about your grill prowess. Grilled Kalamata Olives (page 61) are especially fun to prepare with your guests surrounding the grill area.

Many of the dips and spreads in this chapter will keep fresh for several days in the refrigerator, ready to be brought out on a weeknight and nibbled on when you arrive home from work. The Hummus with Grilled

Garlic (page 70) and the Cannellini Bean Spread with Grilled
Red Peppers (page 71) will both keep for several days in the
refrigerator, so they are great choices to enjoy as a pre-prepared,
instant snack. We must remember to pamper ourselves with
good food and make it easily accessible to family and friends,
rather than just saving it for special occasions.

Lettuce Wraps
with Grilled Red Peppers and Kalamata Olives

This appetizer has a Greek theme and is easy to prepare any time of the year. It is low in carbohydrates but big in flavor.

INGREDIENTS

1 large red bell pepper

12 large butter lettuce leaves

1/2 cup (115 grams) crème fraîche

4 ounces (115 grams) soft goat
    cheese

1/4 cup (25 grams) chopped
    kalamata olives

6 teaspoons snipped fresh
    oregano

Several grinds black pepper,
    to taste

Yield: 6 side-dish servings

Preheat the grill to high. Place the bell pepper directly on the grill and grill for 10 to 15 minutes, turning frequently. (The skin will be charred black.) Transfer the pepper to a plastic or paper bag, close the bag, and set aside for about 15 minutes.

Meanwhile, wash the lettuce leaves, carefully spin them dry in a salad spinner or shake off the water, and place them on a towel to dry. Set aside.

When the bell pepper is cool enough to handle, peel off the charred skin and discard the seeds, stem, and white membrane. Chop the pepper and place it in medium bowl along with the crème fraîche and goat cheese. Mix with a wooden spoon to combine. Add the olives, oregano, and black pepper and then mix to combine.

Place a lettuce leaf, cupped side up, on a work surface. Spoon one-twelfth of the pepper mixture slightly off-center on the leaf. Wrap in the sides of the leaf and place seam side down on a serving plate. Repeat the process with the remaining leaves and pepper mixture. If not serving immediately, you can hold them over in the refrigerator for an hour or so.

Purple Figs
Stuffed with Blue Cheese

INGREDIENTS

8 large, firm, ripe purple figs

1/2 cup (45 grams) crumbled
  blue cheese

4 thin slices rustic country loaf
  bread, cut into triangles

This simple appetizer is a seasonal treat, so prepare and serve it often at the height of fig season in late summer. Choose figs that are firmly ripe so that they hold up on the grill. There may be a small amount of the filling left over after you fill the figs. Spread it on bread and enjoy while you grill the figs.

Preheat the grill to medium-high. Cut the stem end from each fig about one-third of the way down and set aside. Hollow out the seed pulp and place in a small bowl. Add the blue cheese to the pulp and mix to combine. Carefully stuff the cheese mixture back into the hollowed-out figs and put the reserved stem end on top of each fig.

Place the figs upright on the grill rack and place the rack on the grill. Grill for about 5 minutes, until the cheese begins to melt and the caps start to rise.

Meanwhile, place the bread on the grill to toast for 2 to 4 minutes, turning as necessary. Continue to grill the figs for about 2 minutes, then carefully remove using a spatula and tongs. (Do not squeeze the figs too much, or you will force the filling out.) Place 2 figs on each serving plate and arrange grilled bread alongside. Serve immediately.

Yield: 4 side-dish servings

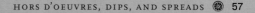

Grilled Spinach Rolls
Stuffed with Tofu and Feta

INGREDIENTS

12 large leaves spinach or chard

5 ounces (140 grams) firm-style
  silken tofu

3/4 cup (115 grams) crumbled feta
  cheese

1/4 teaspoon granulated garlic

1/8 teaspoon freshly grated nutmeg

Several grinds black pepper, to
  taste

12 long, thick fresh chives

1/2 teaspoon olive oil

2 lemons, cut in wedges

Choose large spinach leaves or use early spring Swiss chard for this recipe. The preparation is simple and may be done in advance. Prepare the rolls as an appetizer for a grill party or serve them as a side dish.

Preheat the grill to medium-high. Wash the spinach or chard and remove the thick stems, taking care not to tear the leaves. Pat them dry with paper towels.

Rinse the tofu and pat dry with paper towels. Cut the tofu into cubes and place in a food processor along with the feta cheese, garlic, nutmeg, and black pepper. Pulse to combine. (The resulting mixture should still be a bit lumpy.) Place a spinach leaf on a work surface and spoon one-twelfth of the filling into the center, tuck in the sides, and roll up. Tie one of the chives around the bundle to secure it. Repeat this process to make the rest of the rolls.

Coat your hands with the olive oil and gently rub each roll. Place them on a cold grill tray, then place the tray on the grill. Grill for about 8 to 10 minutes, turning, to heat through. Serve immediately, passing the lemon.

Yield: 6 side-dish servings

Eggplant with Ricotta
and Tomato Coulis

I love to serve this appetizer during the summer when all of the ingredients are in season. Pass a good crusty bread to mop up the sauce and serve a crisp red wine.

INGREDIENTS

2 medium eggplants

$^1/_2$ cup (120 milliliters) olive oil

2 cups (500 grams) ricotta cheese

6 teaspoons minced fresh oregano

$^1/_4$ teaspoon salt

Several grinds black pepper,
   to taste

2 cups (470 milliliters) Tomato
   Coulis (page 24)

Preheat the grill to medium-high. Remove the stem ends of the eggplants. Cut them lengthwise into $^1/_2$-inch slices. Use a pastry brush to coat one side with some of the olive oil and place oil sides down on the grill. Grill for 4 to 6 minutes, brush the top sides with the remaining oil, turn, and grill for 3 to 5 minutes. (The eggplant should be slightly soft with grill marks but not completely blackened.) Remove the eggplant to a cutting board.

Meanwhile, combine the ricotta cheese with the oregano, salt, and black pepper in a bowl.

Place the Tomato Coulis in a small saucepan and heat over medium-low.

Working with one slice of eggplant at a time, place some of the ricotta mixture in the center and roll over the ends. Repeat with the remaining slices. Place the eggplant rolls, seam side down, on a platter or individual serving plates. Pour the warm Tomato Coulis over the top and serve immediately.

Yield: 8 side-dish servings

Basil-Pesto Stuffed Mushrooms

INGREDIENTS

12 large button mushrooms

1 tablespoon (14 milliliters) olive oil

$^1/_2$ cup (55 grams) bread crumbs

$^1/_4$ cup (65 grams) Basil Pesto (page 23)

$^1/_4$ cup (60 grams) non-fat plain yogurt

2 tablespoons (30 grams) low-fat sour cream

3 teaspoons pine nuts, chopped

Serve this easy, elegant appetizer hot off the grill, placed on a platter, drizzled with a bit of olive oil and garnished with some fresh basil leaves. Or you can pack the mushrooms in a container in a single layer and enjoy them on your next picnic.

Brush any dirt from the mushrooms and carefully snap off the stem ends. Reserve the stems for another use. Lightly oil the mushroom tops with the olive oil and set them aside on a platter.

Preheat the grill to medium-high. Place the bread crumbs, Basil Pesto, yogurt, and sour cream in a bowl and mix to combine. Spoon equal amounts into the cavity of each mushroom and top with the pine nuts. Place the mushrooms on a grill rack and transfer to the grill. Grill for 10 minutes until the mushrooms are moist and tender. Transfer the mushrooms to a platter or individual small plates. Serve immediately.

Yield: 12 side-dish servings

Grilled Kalamata Olives

INGREDIENTS

2 cups (200 grams) kalamata
  olives

1 tablespoon (14 milliliters)
  olive oil

3 teaspoons minced fresh thyme

This simple dish is a common appetizer served in countries throughout the Mediterranean. Any salt-cured black olive may be used, although the kalamata variety is commonly available. If you are going to use the olives as an ingredient in a recipe, pit them first, then proceed with grilling.

Place the olives in a bowl and drizzle with the olive oil. Sprinkle with the thyme and toss to combine. Marinate for about 45 minutes, tossing occasionally.

Preheat the grill to medium-high with a smoker box in place. Put the olives in a grilling basket and grill for 4 to 5 minutes, stirring frequently. (The olives will darken slightly and wrinkle.)

Remove the olives from the grill and place in a serving bowl with a smaller bowl for the pits alongside. Let the olives cool for several minutes before serving because the pits will be very hot.

Yield: 16 side-dish servings

Mushrooms Stuffed with
Couscous, Mint Pesto, and Walnuts

INGREDIENTS

$^1/_2$ cup (60 grams) chopped raw, unsalted walnuts

$^1/_3$ cup (60 grams) uncooked couscous

12 large button mushrooms

1 tablespoon (14 milliliters) olive oil

$^1/_2$ cup Mint Pesto (page 23)

$^1/_3$ cup (80 grams) non-fat plain yogurt

2 tablespoons (30 grams) low-fat sour cream

A stuffed mushroom is the perfect composed appetizer. This one is best served on a small plate with a fork.

Place the walnuts in a single layer in a dry heavy-bottomed skillet over medium-high heat. Shake the pan frequently until the nuts are golden brown and emit a wonderful roasted aroma. Immediately remove the walnuts from the pan and set aside.

Place $^2/_3$ cups (150 milliliters) water in a small saucepan on the stovetop over high heat and bring to a boil. Add the couscous, stir, cover, and remove from the heat. Set aside for 5 minutes.

Preheat the grill to medium-high. Brush any dirt from the mushrooms and carefully snap off the stem ends. Reserve the stems for another use. Lightly oil the mushroom tops with the olive oil and set them aside on a platter, gill side up.

Stir the Mint Pesto, yogurt, and sour cream into the couscous. Fill each mushroom cavity with equal amounts of the couscous mixture and top with the toasted walnuts.

Place the mushrooms on a grill rack and transfer to the grill. Grill for 10 minutes, until the mushrooms are moist and tender. Transfer the mushrooms to a platter or individual small plates. Serve immediately.

Yield: 12 side-dish servings

Grilled Artichokes
with Lemon Butter and Summer Savory

INGREDIENTS

2 medium artichokes

I teaspoon (14 milliliters) olive oil

2 tablespoons (28 grams)
   unsalted butter

I teaspoon minced fresh summer
   savory

Pinch salt

I tablespoon (14 milliliters) freshly
   squeezed lemon juice

8 slices Italian-style country bread

Placing these artichokes on the grill to finish the cooking gives them a delightful smoky flavor. You may brush the artichokes with olive oil or use a spray oil to coat them. Pass fresh crusty bread to sop up the sauce.

Snap off the small, tough outer leaves at the base of the artichokes. Trim off about $^1/_4$ inch of the sharp points from the mid-range leaves and from the top. Trim about $^1/_2$ inch from the base of the stem. Put a steamer rack in a large saucepan that has a tight-fitting lid and place the artichokes on the rack, leaves pointing down. Add several inches of water to the saucepan and cover tightly. Place the saucepan on the stovetop and bring the water to a boil, reduce the heat to medium, and steam for about 25 minutes until the bottoms of the artichokes are tender but not soft. Remove the artichokes from the saucepan to a cutting board. Let the artichokes cool for several minutes. Cut each artichoke in half lengthwise with a sharp knife. Spoon out and discard the choke (the fuzzy fibers), leaving the leaves attached to the bottom.

   Preheat the grill to medium-high. Rub the cut sides of the artichokes with the olive oil and place cut sides down on the grill. Grill for 1 to 2 minutes on each side to heat through and create grill marks.

   Meanwhile, melt the butter in a small pan on the stovetop and add the savory and salt. Remove the pan from the heat and stir in the lemon juice. Arrange the artichokes on a serving platter or individual appetizer plates. Drizzle with the butter mixture and set aside for a few minutes so some of the butter will soak in. Serve while still warm, with the bread.

Yield: 4 side-dish servings

Crostini
with Fresh Tomatoes, Basil, and Garlic

INGREDIENTS

3 medium tomatoes

I cup (45 grams) fresh basil

2 tablespoons (15 grams) chopped capers

2 tablespoons (28 milliliters) extra-virgin olive oil

2 teaspoons freshly squeezed lemon juice

3 cloves garlic, minced

Pinch salt

I baguette (I pound)

Crostini—toasted bread slices—are wonderful to prepare during the summertime on the grill. All of the topping ingredients you'll need are in season, and your guests can join in the preparation. I like to use a baguette, but you may use another shape of bread and cut the slices into smaller pieces.

Cut the tomatoes in half crosswise and squeeze out the seed pockets. Cut out and discard the stem ends. Dice the tomatoes and place in a bowl.

Chop the basil or roll up the leaves and cut chiffonade-style (see page 16 for this technique) into paper-thin shreds. Add the basil to the bowl along with the capers and toss to combine.

In another bowl, whisk together the olive oil, lemon juice, garlic, and salt. Drizzle over the tomato mixture and toss to combine. Set aside at room temperature until ready to serve.

Meanwhile, preheat the grill to medium. Cut the baguette into $1/2$-inch slices. Arrange the bread on the grill rack in a single layer. Grill for 1 to 2 minutes per side until the bread is lightly browned and crisp on the outside, but still soft and chewy on the inside, creating perfect crostini. Set aside.

To serve, place a spoonful of the tomato mixture on top of each slice of crostini and serve on a platter or allow your guests to serve themselves, mounding the tomato mixture onto single slices of crostini.

Yield: 12 side-dish servings

Crostini
with Grilled Zucchini and Eggplant

INGREDIENTS

4 medium zucchini

2 Japanese eggplants

2 tablespoons (28 milliliters) olive oil

4 pear tomatoes

3 tablespoons (45 milliliters) extra-virgin olive oil

2 tablespoons (28 milliliters) balsamic vinegar

3 teaspoons minced fresh oregano

3 teaspoons minced fresh basil

1 teaspoon minced fresh thyme

$1/8$ teaspoon salt

Several grinds black pepper, to taste

2 baguettes (1 pound each)

During the summer months, every gardener who has planted zucchini and eggplant is constantly looking for new ways to prepare the yields from these bountiful crops. You may cut this recipe in half if you are not entertaining guests or simply keep the leftovers to enjoy the next day.

Preheat the grill to medium-high. Remove the ends from the zucchini and discard. Slice the zucchini lengthwise. Remove the stem ends from the eggplants and discard. Slice the eggplants lengthwise. Place the zucchini and eggplants in a plastic bag and drizzle with the olive oil. Twist the bag to seal, allowing some air to remain in the bag. Toss gently to coat the vegetables evenly. Place the zucchini and eggplants on the grill and grill for 8 to 10 minutes, turning frequently. Remove all of the zucchini and eggplant from the grill and set aside on a cutting board to cool for several minutes. When the zucchini and eggplant are cool enough to handle, chop and set aside.

Meanwhile, remove the cores from the tomatoes and discard. Cut the tomatoes in half and gently squeeze to remove the seed pockets. Chop the tomatoes and set aside in a large bowl. Add the chopped zucchini and eggplant.

In a small bowl, whisk together the extra-virgin olive oil, balsamic vinegar, oregano, basil, thyme, salt, and black pepper. Drizzle over the tomato and grilled vegetable mixture and toss to combine.

Cut the baguette into $1/2$-inch slices. Arrange the slices on the grill rack in a single layer. Grill for about 2 minutes per side until the bread is lightly browned and crisp on the outside, but still soft and chewy on the inside, creating perfect crostini. Set aside.

To serve, place a spoonful of the vegetable mixture on top of each slice of crostini and serve on a platter or allow your guests to serve themselves, mounding the vegetable mixture onto single slices of crostini.

Yield: 24 side-dish servings

Bruschetta

Bruschetta is Italian-style garlic bread. Be sure to choose a good, fruity olive oil for the most flavorful results.

INGREDIENTS

6 tablespoons (90 milliliters)
   extra-virgin olive oil

4 cloves garlic, minced

1 loaf thick-crusted bread
   (1 pound)

Preheat the grill to medium. Whisk together the olive oil and garlic in a small bowl. Set aside.

If using a baguette-shaped loaf, cut it into $^1/_2$-inch slices. If using a dome-shaped loaf, cut it in half, then cut each half into $^1/_2$-inch slices. Place the bread on the grill. Cook for about 2 minutes per side until the bread is lightly browned and crisp on the outside, but still soft and chewy on the inside. Remove the bread from the grill and brush one side with the oil and garlic mixture. Serve immediately.

Yield: 12 side-dish servings

Garlic Jam

Cooking whole garlic bulbs transforms the garlic cloves into a pungent paste consistency—or jam—that can be spread on bread or used as an ingredient in many recipes. The smoky, mellow garlic flavor is quite distinct from the taste of raw garlic.

INGREDIENTS

2 large bulbs fresh garlic

$^1/_4$ teaspoon olive oil

8 sprigs fresh flat-leaf parsley

I loaf thick-crusted bread, sliced
   (I pound)

Preheat the grill to medium. Rub the papery skin from the garlic, but do not break them into individual cloves. Cut about $^1/_2$ inch off the pointed top ends of the bulbs and rub the cut surfaces with the olive oil. Place the garlic bulbs, cut sides up, in a covered clay or glass baking dish and place on the grill. (You could wrap the garlic in foil. Then place the foil packet on a baking stone or on baking bricks so the garlic cooks but does not burn on the bottom.) Grill for about 45 minutes. When the garlic feels very soft when gently squeezed, remove from the grill. Place the garlic on a serving dish and let cool for several minutes.

Gently pull the garlic cloves apart, leaving them attached to the base of the bulbs. Place the garlic on a serving platter and garnish with the parsley. Place the bread in a basket. To remove the garlic from the skin, squeeze a clove from the bottom, allowing the garlic jam to slide out from the cut end onto the slices of bread. Pass a lot of napkins because this is finger food.

Yield: 12 side-dish servings

Grilled Pita Triangles

INGREDIENTS

6 rounds whole wheat pita bread

4 tablespoons (60 milliliters)
  olive oil

These pita bread "chips" are great by themselves, or they are also wonderful with a variety of dips or spreads. Watch carefully while the chips are grilling because they will burn to a crisp if unattended.

Preheat the grill to medium. Cut each pita-bread round into quarters, then separate the layers to create 8 triangles per round. Lightly brush or spray the pita bread with the olive oil and place directly on the grill. Grill for about 5 minutes, turning frequently until both sides are slightly toasted. Place in a basket and serve.

Yield: 24 side-dish servings

Hummus
with Grilled Garlic

Hummus—garbanzo-bean spread—has many variations. This is my favorite variation. Serve with Grilled Pita Triangles (page 69), sesame crackers, or fresh vegetables. This spread will keep refrigerated for several days.

INGREDIENTS

1 bulb garlic

1/4 teaspoon olive oil

2 cups (325 grams) cooked garbanzo beans

1/3 cup (75 milliliters) freshly squeezed lemon juice

1/4 cup (60 grams) toasted sesame tahini

2 tablespoons (28 milliliters) extra-virgin olive oil

2 green onions, minced

1/2 teaspoon salt

Preheat the grill to medium. Rub the papery skin from the garlic, but do not break it into individual cloves. Cut about 1/2 inch off the pointed top end of the bulb and rub the cut surface with the olive oil. Place the garlic bulb, cut side up, in a covered clay or glass baking dish and place on the grill, and grill for about 45 minutes. (You could wrap the garlic in foil. Then place the foil packet on a baking stone or on baking bricks so the garlic cooks but does not burn on the bottom.) When the garlic feels very soft when gently squeezed, remove from the grill. When cool enough to handle, squeeze the garlic paste from the individual cloves into a small bowl and set aside.

Place the garbanzo beans, lemon juice, tahini, extra-virgin olive oil, and 1 tablespoon (14 milliliters) water in a blender or food processor and puree until smooth. (Add a tablespoon or two of water if the mixture is too thick.) Add the green onions, grilled garlic, and salt, and pulse to combine.

Transfer the hummus to a serving dish and serve immediately or refrigerate for up to several days. Serve at room temperature.

Yield: 18 side-dish servings

Cannellini Bean Spread
with Grilled Red Pepper

INGREDIENTS

1 large red bell pepper

15 ounces (430 grams) canned cannellini beans

1 tablespoon (14 milliliters) extra-virgin olive oil

1 tablespoon (14 milliliters) fresh-squeezed lemon juice

6 teaspoons minced fresh basil

1/2 teaspoon salt

You can find dried cannellini beans in any natural food store or Italian market and can easily soak and cook them. For convenience, they are also available precooked, sold in 15-ounce cans in many markets, and that's what I used in this recipe. Serve this spread on crackers or bread. It is also delicious as a sandwich spread.

Preheat the grill to high. Place the bell pepper directly on the grill and grill for 10 to 15 minutes, turning frequently. (The skin will be charred black.) Transfer the pepper to a plastic or paper bag, close the bag, and set aside for about 15 minutes. When the pepper is cool enough to handle, peel off the charred skin and discard the stem, seeds, and white membrane. Coarsely chop.

Place the grilled pepper, cannellini beans, 2 tablespoons (28 milliliters) water, olive oil, lemon juice, basil, and salt in a food processor. Pulse to combine. Transfer to a serving bowl and serve immediately or refrigerate overnight.

Yield: 10 appetizer servings

Grilled Eggplant Spread

INGREDIENTS

2 medium eggplants

4 green onions, minced

2 cloves garlic, minced

$^1/_4$ cup (15 grams) minced fresh
parsley

6 teaspoons minced fresh oregano

$^1/_4$ teaspoon salt

Several grinds black pepper, to
taste

$^1/_4$ cup (60 milliliters) extra-virgin
olive oil

3 tablespoons (45 milliliters)
freshly squeezed lemon juice

*I first enjoyed a version of this dish, also called baba ghanouj, on the
Greek island of Mykonos. This recipe may not be authentic, but it is delicious and duplicates the flavors I savored that day. Serve this spread as an
appetizer with crusty bread or as a salad mounded in a butter lettuce leaf.*

Preheat the grill to medium-high. Place the eggplants on the grill
and grill for about 1 hour. Turn the eggplants several times as they
cook. (The skins will become charred and the eggplants will
become very soft.) Remove the eggplants from the grill and set
aside to cool. When the eggplants are cool enough to handle, cut
off the stem ends and peel away the skin. Drain off any liquid.
Coarsely chop the eggplant and transfer it to a food processor. Add
the green onions, garlic, parsley, oregano, salt, and black pepper.
Pulse to combine, achieving a chunky—not perfectly smooth—
texture. Add the olive oil and lemon juice and pulse to combine.
Transfer to a serving bowl and serve immediately or allow the
flavors to blend at room temperature for an hour or so.

Yield: 12 appetizer servings

Jicama and Grilled Red Bell Peppers

INGREDIENTS

1 large red bell pepper

1 small jícama

2 tablespoons (28 milliliters)
   freshly squeezed lime juice

1 teaspoon mild chili powder

1/8 teaspoon salt

This refreshing appetizer is delightfully simple. It can be prepared ahead of time and refrigerated until serving. One of the wonderful qualities of jícama is that it retains its crispness for several days—even after it is cut.

Preheat the grill to high. Place the bell pepper directly on the grill and grill for 10 to 15 minutes, turning frequently. (The skin will be charred black.) Transfer the pepper to a plastic or paper bag, close the bag, and set aside for about 15 minutes. When the pepper is cool enough to handle, peel off the charred skin and discard the seeds, stem, and white membrane. Dice the pepper and set aside.

Meanwhile, peel the jícama and cut it in half from stem to root. Place each piece cut side down on a cutting board and cut into 1/4-inch slices. Place the slices in a bowl and drizzle with the lime juice. Toss to combine.

On a pretty plate, make a ring of overlapping slices of jícama, retaining the lime juice in the bowl. Mound the diced pepper in the center of the ring. Drizzle the reserved lime juice evenly over the jícama and bell pepper, then dust the jícama with the chili powder and salt.

Serve immediately or cover with plastic wrap and refrigerate overnight. Place a small fork on the plate before serving. To serve, allow diners to place a small mound of bell pepper on a jícama slice and eat with their fingers.

Yield: 8 appetizer servings

CHAPTER 5

Salads and Side Dishes

Grilling adds a delicious flavor to vegetable side dishes and, surprisingly, many salads as well. And it's so convenient to create the entire meal out at the grill rather than running back and forth to the stove. You'll be delighted with the range of salad and side-dish recipes in this chapter.

Spring gardens and local farmers' markets bring us an abundance of fresh lettuce leaves, thus providing the perfect mix of greens. During the summer and winter months—depending on your climate—you can grow a fresh salad mix or rely on the world market to provide for your culinary needs through your local greengrocer.

Some of the recipes in this chapter call for tossed leaf greens with grilled vegetables or fruits. Many should be enjoyed at the peak of the season for the particular ingredient, like the Spinach Salad with Grilled Peaches and Gorgonzola Cheese (page 82), Red Lettuce Salad with Grilled Beets and Goat Cheese (page 79), or the Iceberg Lettuce with Grilled Figs and Creamy Blue Cheese Dressing (page 84). Ingredients for other salads, such as Caesar Salad with Smoky Grilled Tofu (page 83) or Fresh Greens with Grilled Hearts of Palm (page 78), can be prepared year-round. The dressings rely on a good olive oil and fresh lemon juice or wine vinegars, along with minced fresh herbs.

Not all of the salads in this chapter call for greens. Some rely on more hearty ingredients, like beans or pasta, as the base. Enjoy the Corn, Black Bean, and Avocado Salad (page 86) or the Pasta Salad with Grilled Radicchio and Sweet Peppers (page 87) all year. Many of these salads can be a light meal all by themselves when served with bread, crackers, or chips.

I think of side-dish vegetables as seasonal for the most part. Spring has arrived when the first locally grown asparagus shows up at the farmers' market. You'll want to prepare the Asparagus with Watercress Sauce (page 90) often and consider serving it as part of a spring or Easter buffet. The summer season graces us with an abundance of vegetables, most of which are delicious when prepared on the grill. Grilling corn in its husk allows the kernels to steam and become tender-crisp—and no flavor is lost to the boiling pot of water! White Corn with Chili Butter (page 96) is sure to become a seasonal favorite. Grilled zucchini is an old standby, so be sure to try the Summer Squashes with Lemon Basil (page 93). When you include the Aussie Chips with Sweet Chili Sauce (page 100) and Grilled Red Potatoes (page 98) in your repertoire, you have seasonless side-dish selections coming hot from your grill.

Grilled Endive Salad
with Golden Raisins

Endive is a slightly bitter lettuce that is firm enough to stand up to the heat of the grill. The leaves wilt slightly and take on the flavor of the fire.

INGREDIENTS

1/4 cup (35 grams) pine nuts

3 tablespoons (45 milliliters) extra-virgin olive oil

1 tablespoon (14 milliliters) balsamic vinegar

1/2 teaspoon honey

1/2 teaspoon Dijon mustard

Pinch salt

Several grinds black pepper, to taste

2 Belgian endives, halved lengthwise

1 tablespoon (14 milliliters) olive oil

6 cups (170 grams) loosely packed torn red lettuce leaves

1/4 cup (35 grams) golden raisins

Place a single layer of pine nuts in a small cast-iron skillet on the stovetop over medium-high heat. Shake the pan frequently. (The nuts will become slightly golden and emit a nutty aroma.) Remove the nuts from the pan and set aside until needed.

In a small bowl, whisk together the extra-virgin olive oil, balsamic vinegar, honey, mustard, salt, and black pepper. Set the dressing aside.

Meanwhile, preheat the grill to medium-high. Use a pastry brush to brush both sides of the endive with some of the olive oil. Place the endive on the grill, cut sides down. Cook for about 2 minutes, baste with some more of the oil, and turn with tongs. Continue to cook for about 2 more minutes. (The endive will wilt slightly and develop grill marks.) Remove the endive from the grill.

Place the lettuce in a large bowl and drizzle with the dressing. Toss to combine. Distribute between 4 salad plates. Place one grilled endive half atop the lettuce on each plate. Sprinkle with equal amounts of raisins and pine nuts. Serve immediately.

Yield: 4 side-dish servings

Mixed Greens
with Grilled Summer Vegetables and Blue Cheese

INGREDIENTS

1 medium yellow crookneck squash

1 medium zucchini

1 Japanese eggplant

1 tablespoon (14 milliliters) olive oil

1/4 cup (60 milliliters) extra-virgin olive oil

2 tablespoons (28 milliliters) red wine vinegar

1 teaspoon Dijon mustard

1/2 teaspoon crushed garlic

Several grinds black pepper, to taste

6 cups (170 grams) mixed greens

1 medium tomato, sliced

1/4 cup (35 grams) crumbled blue cheese

The abundance of summer produce inspires many of my recipes. Here, cooking the vegetables with a smoker box on the grill adds a unique flavor to this salad. The blue cheese complements the flavors.

Preheat the grill to medium-high. Remove the ends from the crookneck squash and zucchini and discard. Slice the squashes lengthwise. Remove the end from the eggplant and discard. Slice the eggplant lengthwise. Place the squashes and eggplant in a plastic bag and drizzle with the olive oil. Twist the bag to seal, allowing some air to remain in the bag. Toss gently to coat the vegetables evenly. Remove the squashes and eggplant from the bag and place them on the grill. Grill for 8 to 10 minutes, turning frequently. Remove the squashes and eggplant from the grill and place on a cutting board. Cool for several minutes, then cut into matchstick slices.

Meanwhile, place the extra-virgin olive oil, red wine vinegar, mustard, garlic, and black pepper in a bowl and whisk to combine.

Place the mixed greens in a large bowl and drizzle with half of the dressing, reserving the remaining dressing. Toss well to coat the leaves. Distribute the lettuce equally between 4 chilled salad plates. Arrange the tomato around the edge of each plate and place equal amounts of matchstick vegetable slices over the top. Drizzle with the remaining dressing. Top with the blue cheese and serve immediately.

Yield: 4 side-dish servings

Fresh Greens with
Grilled Hearts of Palm

INGREDIENTS

7.75 ounces (220 grams) canned
  hearts of palm

1 tablespoon (14 milliliters) olive oil

2 tablespoons (28 milliliters) freshly
  squeezed lime juice

2 teaspoons minced fresh oregano

8 cups (225 grams) loosely packed
  mixed salad greens

1 lemon cucumber, peeled and
  chopped

12 cherry tomatoes, halved

1/4 cup (60 milliliters) extra-virgin
  olive oil

3 teaspoons minced fresh flat-leaf
  parsley

1 teaspoon Dijon mustard

Pinch granulated garlic

You can find the ingredients to make this refreshing salad at any time of year. Hearts of palm are sold in cans in most supermarkets. The smaller stalks are always tender, but the larger ones can be a bit tough. If the can you purchase has larger ones in it, peel away the outer layers before you marinate them.

Drain the hearts of palm and place in a shallow dish.

In a separate bowl, whisk together the olive oil, 1 tablespoon of the lime juice, and 1 teaspoon of the oregano. Pour over the hearts of palm and marinate for about 15 minutes. Roll the hearts of palm to coat as they marinate.

Preheat the grill to medium-high. Meanwhile, place the greens in a medium bowl. Add the cucumber and tomatoes.

In a small bowl, whisk together the extra-virgin olive oil, the remaining 1 tablespoon lime juice, the parsley, the remaining 1 teaspoon oregano, the mustard, and garlic to make a dressing. Set aside.

Place the hearts of palm in a grill basket on the grill and grill for about 5 minutes, turning frequently, until heated through and seared with grill marks. Remove from the grill to a cutting board and cut into thick slices. Toss the salad greens with the dressing and distribute equally between 4 salad plates. Top with equal amounts of grilled hearts of palm and serve.

Yield: 4 side-dish servings

Red Lettuce Salad
with Grilled Beets and Goat Cheese

INGREDIENTS

1 pound (455 grams) small fresh beets

$^1/_3$ cup (75 milliliters) Raspberry Vinegar Marinade (page 28)

6 cups (170 grams) loosely packed torn red lettuce leaves

3 tablespoons (45 milliliters) extra-virgin olive oil

1 tablespoon (14 milliliters) raspberry vinegar

2 ounces (55 grams) soft goat cheese

To make this beautiful and delicious salad, purchase small, fresh spring beets, measuring the weight with the tops removed. If you can find yellow beets, mix them with the red variety. The Raspberry Vinegar Marinade seasons the beets perfectly.

Peel the beets and cut them into $^1/_4$-inch slices. Place them in a bowl with the Raspberry Vinegar Marinade and toss to coat. Allow the beets to marinate for about 45 minutes, tossing occasionally.

Preheat the grill to medium. Place the beets on the grill and grill for about 15 minutes, turning several times, until fork-tender. Remove the beets from the grill to a cutting board. Cut the beets into strips and set aside to cool.

Meanwhile, place the lettuce in a shallow bowl.

In a small bowl, whisk together the olive oil and raspberry vinegar. Pour over the lettuce and toss to coat. Place equal amounts of lettuce on 4 serving plates. Arrange the beet strips on top and use a fork to crumble the goat cheese over the beets.

Yield: 4 side-dish servings

Spinach Salad with
Spiced Walnuts and Fire-Roasted Red Bell Pepper

INGREDIENTS

1 medium red bell pepper

6 cups (180 grams) loosely packed baby spinach leaves

1/3 cup (40 grams) chopped raw, unsalted walnuts

2 teaspoons freshly squeezed lime juice

1/4 teaspoon granulated garlic

1/4 teaspoon chili powder

1/4 teaspoon salt

2 tablespoons (28 milliliters) orange juice

1 tablespoon (14 milliliters) apple cider vinegar

1 tablespoon (14 milliliters) olive oil

1/2 small red onion, thinly sliced

Several grinds black pepper, to taste

6 teaspoons minced fresh cilantro

This composed salad is perfect for a fancy dinner, stunning in both visual appeal and flavor. The seasonings suggest Tex-Mex cuisine, so pair this with fajitas or quesadillas as the main course.

Preheat the grill to high. Place the bell pepper directly on the grill and cook for 10 to 15 minutes, turning frequently. Cook until the skin is charred black. Transfer the pepper to a plastic or paper bag, close the bag, and set aside for about 15 minutes. When the pepper is cool enough to handle, peel off the charred skin and discard the seeds, stem, and white membrane. Slice the pepper into thin 1-inch strips and set them aside.

Wash the spinach and discard the stems. Dry the spinach and coarsely tear into bite-size pieces. Place the spinach in a large bowl and set aside.

Heat a dry heavy-bottomed skillet over medium heat on the stovetop and toast the walnuts for about 5 minutes, shaking the pan frequently. When the walnuts are golden brown, place them in a small bowl and toss with the lime juice while they are still warm. Sprinkle on the garlic, chili powder, and 1/8 teaspoon of the salt. Toss to distribute evenly and set aside.

Whisk together the orange juice, apple cider vinegar, vinegar, olive oil, and the remaining 1/8 teaspoon salt in a small bowl.

Toss together the spinach, onion, and orange juice mixture. Distribute evenly among 6 chilled salad plates. Top the spinach with the bell pepper strips and sprinkle with the spiced nuts. Grind a little black pepper on each one and sprinkle evenly with the cilantro. Serve immediately.

Yield: 6 side-dish servings

Spinach Salad
with Grilled Peaches and Gorgonzola Cheese

INGREDIENTS

3 tablespoons (45 milliliters)
   extra-virgin olive oil

1 tablespoon (14 milliliters)
   raspberry vinegar

1/4 teaspoon crushed garlic

Pinch salt

Several grinds black pepper, to taste

1/4 cup (30 grams) chopped pecans

6 cups (180 grams) loosely packed
   baby spinach leaves

2 medium yellow peaches

1 ounce (28 grams) crumbled
   Gorgonzola cheese

The sweet peaches and sharp Gorgonzola cheese go together well in this distinctive spinach salad.

Place the olive oil, raspberry vinegar, garlic, salt, and black pepper in a small bowl and whisk to combine into a dressing. Set aside.

Place the pecans in a small skillet on the stovetop over medium-high heat. Shake the pan frequently until the pecans emit a roasted aroma. Remove the pecans from the pan and set aside until needed.

Wash the spinach and discard the stems. Dry the spinach and coarsely tear into bite-size pieces. Place the spinach in a shallow bowl and toss with the dressing just before serving.

When ready to serve, preheat the grill to medium-high. Cut each peach into 8 slices. Place the slices in a grill basket and put it on the grill. Grill for about 2 minutes, then turn and grill for about 2 more minutes.

Put equal portions of spinach on 4 salad plates. Top the spinach with peach slices, arranged around the perimeter of the plate. Sprinkle each salad with equal amounts of Gorgonzola cheese and pecans. Serve immediately.

Yield: 4 side-dish servings

Caesar Salad
with Smoky Grilled Tofu

INGREDIENTS

14 ounces (400 grams) extra-firm
   tofu

3 tablespoons (45 milliliters) olive oil

1 1/2 tablespoons (21 milliliters)
   balsamic vinegar

1 large head romaine lettuce

1 medium egg

2 cloves garlic, minced

3 tablespoons (45 milliliters) freshly
   squeezed lemon juice

1 tablespoon (14 milliliters)
   vegetarian Worcestershire sauce

1/2 cup (120 milliliters) extra-virgin
   olive oil

1 cup (30 grams) croutons

1/2 cup (50 grams) finely grated
   Parmesan cheese

A good Caesar salad is hard to pass up, and this one, with grilled tofu strips, is a delicious variation on this popular salad. The tofu is pressed to remove the water, then marinated briefly. Most of the oil that is used in the marinade drips off while grilling, producing a delightful flavor.

Preheat the grill to medium-high with a smoker box in place. Drain the tofu and cut the slab in half width-wise to create 2 pieces. Place each piece on a paper towel and cover with another towel. Place a heavy skillet on top to press the excess water from the tofu. After 15 minutes, place the tofu between fresh paper towels and repeat the process.

In a bowl, whisk together the olive oil and balsamic vinegar and pour into a rimmed baking pan. Again, cut the tofu slabs in half width-wise and soak each side in the oil and vinegar mixture. Place the tofu on the hot grill. Grill for about 10 minutes, turning several times. Remove the tofu from the grill and set aside to cool slightly. When the tofu is cool enough to handle, cut into thin strips. Set aside.

Meanwhile, wash and dry the lettuce, then tear it into bite-size pieces, and briefly set it aside in the refrigerator to keep cold and crisp.

In a large bowl, whisk together the egg, garlic, lemon juice, and Worcestershire sauce. Gradually add the extra-virgin olive oil in a thin stream, whisking as you do. Continue to whisk for a minute or two until emulsified. Add the lettuce and toss well to coat with the dressing. Add the croutons and Parmesan cheese and toss again. Arrange equal amounts on chilled salad plates. Top with the strips of tofu and serve immediately.

Yield: 6 side-dish servings

Iceberg Lettuce
with Grilled Figs and Creamy Blue Cheese Dressing

INGREDIENTS

3/4 cup (175 grams) mayonnaise

3/4 cup (100 grams) crumbled
blue cheese

1/4 cup (60 grams) sour cream

2 tablespoons (28 milliliters) red
wine vinegar

1 tablespoon (12 grams) sugar

1/2 teaspoon crushed garlic

1 head iceberg lettuce

12 firm, ripe green figs

The crispness of the iceberg lettuce is perfect for this salad. The green figs with their purple-seeded centers soften as they grill and are delicious with the blue cheese dressing.

Place the mayonnaise, blue cheese, sour cream, red wine vinegar, sugar, and garlic in a bowl and whisk together to make the dressing. (There will be lumps of blue cheese in the creamy mixture.) Set aside in the refrigerator.

Remove the center core from the lettuce and discard. Tear the rest into bite-size pieces, placing equal amounts of lettuce on 6 chilled salad plates. Set aside in the refrigerator.

Preheat the grill to medium-high. Cut off and discard the stem ends and slice the figs in half lengthwise. Place the figs cut sides up (skin sides down) on the grill and grill for about 4 minutes until the centers are soft. Remove the figs from the grill and arrange 4 halves on top of the lettuce on each plate. Spoon equal amounts of blue cheese dressing on each plate and serve immediately.

Yield: 6 side-dish servings

Grilled Tomato Salad
with Fresh Mozzarella Cheese

INGREDIENTS

2 tomatoes

$^1/_2$ teaspoon mild chili powder

$^1/_2$ teaspoon granulated garlic

2 balls fresh mozzarella
   (about 8 ounces/225 grams)

2 tablespoons (28 milliliters)
   extra-virgin olive oil

I teaspoon balsamic vinegar

16 fresh basil leaves

$^1/_4$ teaspoon salt

Several grinds black pepper,
   to taste

This salad is a twist on the classic Italian Insalata di Pomodoro e Mozzarella. *Look for fresh mozzarella cheese packed in water. It is sold at deli counters or specialty food markets.*

Preheat the grill to medium with a smoker box in place. Core the tomatoes and quarter them. Sprinkle the tomatoes with the chili powder and the garlic. Place the tomatoes on the grill and grill for 2 to 3 minutes, then turn them and continue to grill for 2 to 3 minutes. Carefully remove the tomatoes from the grill and set aside.

Cut the mozzarella into $^1/_4$-inch slices. Arrange the grilled tomato wedges on serving plates and place equal amounts of mozzarella slices on each plate. Drizzle with the olive oil, then with the balsamic vinegar.

Stack the basil leaves and cut them crosswise into thin strips. Distribute them on top of the tomato and cheese. Sprinkle with the salt and black pepper, then serve at room temperature.

Yield: 4 side-dish servings

Corn, Black Bean, and Avocado Salad

INGREDIENTS

1/4 cup (60 milliliters) olive oil

1/4 cup (60 milliliters) freshly
squeezed orange juice

3 tablespoons (45 milliliters)
freshly squeezed lime juice

I teaspoon crushed garlic

1/4 teaspoon ground cumin

1/2 teaspoon salt

2 ears yellow corn, not husked

4 cups (860 grams) cooked
black beans

2 Haas avocados, peeled, seeded,
and diced

2 cups (240 grams) peeled and
diced jícama

6 green onions, diced

1/2 cup (8 grams) chopped fresh
cilantro

The colors of this salad are a feast for the eyes, whetting the appetite for the first bite. Serve this as a side dish for a multi-course Tex-Mex theme dinner or as a main dish for 6 with chips and Guacamole (page 48). Haas avocados have pebbled deep green to black skin. This salad is best prepared ahead of time and refrigerated until needed.

To prepare the dressing, whisk together the olive oil, orange juice, lime juice, garlic, cumin, and salt in a small bowl. Set aside.

Place the corn in a plastic bag and fill the bag with water to soak the husks for about 15 minutes. Meanwhile, preheat the grill to high. Remove the corn from the bag of water and place the corn on the grill. Turn the corn every few minutes to evenly blacken all sides of the husks. Grill for 18 to 22 minutes. (The kernels will steam in the husks.) Remove the corn from the grill. Allow the corn to cool for a few minutes, then peel off the husks and remove the silk. Cut the corn from the cob and place in a large bowl.

Drain and rinse the black beans and add them to the corn. Toss in the avocado, jícama, green onions, and cilantro. Drizzle with the dressing and toss. Refrigerate until needed.

Yield: 12 side-dish servings

Pasta Salad with
Grilled Radicchio and Sweet Peppers

INGREDIENTS

1 head radicchio

1 small yellow bell pepper

1 small red bell pepper

2 tablespoons (28 milliliters) olive oil

1 teaspoon crushed garlic

12 ounces (340 grams) penne pasta

2 tablespoons (28 milliliters) extra-virgin olive oil

1 tablespoon (14 milliliters) balsamic vinegar

$1/8$ teaspoon mild chili powder

2 teaspoons minced fresh oregano

3 green onions, minced

Parmesan cheese (optional)

The colors in this salad will entice you before you and your guests even taste it. Radicchio is a member of the chicory family, and it is likely sold in the fresh greens section of your supermarket. This salad is easy to prepare and set aside in the refrigerator until you're ready to serve it.

Preheat the grill to medium. Cut the radicchio into quarters, removing the core section. Core and seed the bell peppers, cutting them into quarters. Place the radicchio and bell peppers in a plastic bag and drizzle with the olive oil and garlic. Twist the bag to seal, allowing some air to remain in the bag. Toss gently to coat the radicchio and peppers evenly.

Place the radicchio and peppers on the grill. Grill the radicchio for 5 to 7 minutes, turning carefully to slightly char all sides. Grill the peppers until limp and slightly charred, 6 to 7 minutes. Remove the radicchio and peppers from the grill and coarsely chop.

Meanwhile, fill a large stockpot with water and place on the stovetop over high heat. Bring to a boil and add the pasta. Cook for 6 to 8 minutes, until al dente. Drain into a colander and rinse with cold water. Drain well and transfer to a shallow serving bowl.

In a bowl, whisk together the extra-virgin olive oil, balsamic vinegar, chili powder, and oregano. Drizzle over the pasta and toss to coat. Add the green onions and the grilled radicchio and peppers, toss to combine, and serve. Pass grated Parmesan cheese, if desired.

Yield: 8 side-dish servings

Pasta Salad with
Grilled Vegetables and Garlic-Chipotle Dressing

INGREDIENTS

2 medium bulbs garlic

3 tablespoons (45 milliliters) plus
   $1/4$ teaspoon olive oil

2 medium yellow onions

I medium eggplant

3 teaspoons coarse salt

3 medium zucchini

12 ounces (340 grams) spiral-
   shaped pasta

6 tablespoons (90 milliliters)
   freshly squeezed lime juice

6 teaspoons minced chipotle
   chiles in adobo

$1/2$ teaspoon salt

$1/4$ cup (60 milliliters) extra-virgin
   olive oil

1 $1/2$ cups (170 grams) crumbled
   queso fresco

This slightly spicy, slightly smoky pasta salad is a summertime favorite. The flavors intermingle to create a Tex-Mex dish. The chipotle chiles in adobo are readily available at most markets.

Preheat the grill to medium. Rub the papery skin from the garlic, but do not break them into individual cloves. Cut about $1/2$ inch off the pointed top ends of the bulbs and rub the cut surfaces with $1/4$ teaspoon of the olive oil. Place the garlic bulbs cut side up in a covered clay or glass baking dish and place on the grill. (You could wrap the garlic in foil. Then place the foil packet on a baking stone or on baking bricks so the garlic cooks but does not burn on the bottom.) Grill for about 45 minutes. When the garlic feel very soft when gently squeezed, remove the garlic from the foil or garlic baker so it can cool.

Meanwhile, trim the ends from the onions and peel them. Cut the onions in half crosswise and lightly brush the cut sides with some of the remaining olive oil. Place the onions on the grill cut sides down and grill for 35 to 45 minutes, turning every 8 to 10 minutes to cook evenly. When the onions are soft and slightly charred, remove from the grill and set aside.

Cut off and discard the stem and bottom ends of the eggplant, but do not peel it. Cut the eggplant crosswise into $1/2$-inch slices. To remove the eggplant's bitter juices, sprinkle both sides of the slices with the salt and place on a rack for about 30 minutes. (The salt will cause the eggplant to "sweat" and release the bitter juices.) Briefly rinse the eggplant slices and blot them dry with paper towels. Brush each side of the eggplant slices with some of the remaining olive oil and place them on the grill. Grill for 5 to 8 minutes until lightly browned, then turn and continue to grill for another 5 to 8 minutes. (The slices should be tender-crisp, not mushy.)

While you are preparing the eggplant, trim off and discard the ends of the zucchini and cut the zucchini in thirds lengthwise. Lightly brush the cut sides with some of the remaining olive oil. Place the zucchini on the grill and grill for 4 to 6 minutes, watching closely and turning frequently. Remove the zucchini from the grill and cool slightly. Coarsely chop the onions, eggplant, and zucchini and place in a large bowl.

Meanwhile, bring several quarts of water to a boil in a large stockpot on the stovetop. Cook the pasta for 6 to 8 minutes until al dente and pour into a large colander. Rinse with cold water and drain well. Transfer the pasta to the bowl with the vegetables and toss to combine.

Squeeze the grilled garlic paste into a blender. Add the lime juice, chipotle chiles, and salt. With the machine running, pour the extra-virgin olive oil into the blender and puree. Pour over the vegetables and pasta and toss to combine. Sprinkle on the queso fresco and toss again. Serve immediately or refrigerate for several hours. Bring to room temperature before serving.

Yield: 10 side-dish servings

Asparagus
with Watercress Sauce

This dish is the signal that spring has finally arrived! Choose the thickest asparagus stalks you can because they're the most succulent and will produce the best results. Enjoy this dish frequently when asparagus and watercress are in season—it is a short one.

INGREDIENTS

3 tablespoons (45 milliliters) extra-virgin olive oil

2 tablespoons (28 milliliters) freshly squeezed lemon juice

$1/8$ teaspoon salt

$1/2$ cup (17 grams) watercress leaves

2 green onions, minced

2 pounds (1 kilogram) fresh asparagus

1 tablespoon (14 milliliters) olive oil

1 hard-boiled egg, peeled and chopped

Combine the extra-virgin olive oil, lemon juice, and salt in a small bowl.

Place the watercress and onions in a blender. Switch on the low setting and add the lemon juice mixture in a slow, steady stream. Blend until you have a smooth sauce. Set aside.

Preheat the grill to medium. Wash the asparagus carefully to remove any traces of soil. Snap off and discard the tough ends. Place the asparagus in a plastic bag and drizzle with the olive oil. Twist the bag to seal, allowing some of the air to remain in the bag. Toss gently to coat the asparagus evenly. Place the asparagus in a grill basket on the grill. Grill for 8 to 10 minutes, turning frequently so the stalks cook but do not burn. (The asparagus should be al dente and slightly charred.) Remove the asparagus from the grill to a serving platter. Spoon the watercress sauce over the top and sprinkle with the chopped egg. Serve hot or at room temperature.

Yield: 10 side-dish servings

Baby Bok Choy
with Lemon Miso Sauce

This simple but flavorful dish is best with the small, tender bok choy, that is usually available in Asian markets.

INGREDIENTS

¹/₄ cup (60 milliliters) freshly
squeezed lemon juice

2 tablespoons (35 grams)
white miso

2 cloves garlic, minced

3 teaspoons cornstarch

I pound (455 grams) baby
bok choy

2 tablespoons (28 milliliters)
toasted sesame oil

Preheat the grill to medium-high. In a small saucepan, whisk together the lemon juice, miso, garlic, and ¹/₄ cup (60 milliliters) water. Place on the stovetop over low heat and cook until steaming.

Place 2 tablespoons (28 milliliters) water in a small jar with a tight-fitting lid and add the cornstarch. Cover tightly and shake to dissolve. Whisk the cornstarch mixture into the saucepan and cook over medium-low heat until thickened, about 1 minute. (Do not overcook or it will get gummy.) Remove the saucepan from the heat and set aside in a warm spot.

Rinse the bok choy and shake to remove some of the water. Cut any larger heads in half lengthwise. Place the bok choy in a plastic bag and drizzle with the sesame oil. Twist the bag to seal, allowing some air to remain in the bag. Toss gently to coat the bok choy evenly. Place the bok choy on the grill and grill for 3 to 5 minutes, turning frequently, until the leaves are limp and slightly charred. Remove the bok choy from the grill and place on a serving platter. Drizzle with the sauce and serve immediately.

Yield: 6 side-dish servings

Summer Squashes
with Lemon Basil

INGREDIENTS

3 medium yellow crookneck
   squash

3 medium zucchini

2 tablespoons (28 milliliters)
   olive oil

I teaspoon crushed garlic

I tablespoon (14 milliliters)
   extra-virgin olive oil

I tablespoon chiffonaded strips
   fresh lemon basil (see page 16
   for this technique)

Use an assortment of summer squashes to create a colorful platter of grilled vegetables. Lemon basil is one of the many varieties that are easy to grow in the summer garden. You may use any type of fresh basil, but I think lemon basil imparts the best flavor to this dish.

Preheat the grill to medium. Remove and discard the stem ends of the squashes and zucchini, and then cut them lengthwise into $1/4$-inch slices. Place the squashes and zucchini in a plastic bag and drizzle with the olive oil and garlic. Twist the bag to seal, allowing some of the air to remain in the bag. Toss gently to coat the squashes and zucchini evenly. Place the squashes and zucchini on the grill and grill for about 10 minutes, until grill marks appear and the slices are tender-crisp, turning twice. Remove the squashes and zucchini and place on a platter. Drizzle with the extra-virgin olive oil and sprinkle with the lemon basil. Serve immediately or at room temperature.

Yield: 6 side-dish servings

Grilled Zucchini

Choose small zucchini for this classic summer side dish because you do not want the watery seed pockets that develop in the larger ones.

INGREDIENTS

6 small zucchini

1 1/2 tablespoons (21 milliliters) olive oil

1 teaspoon crushed garlic

1 tablespoon (14 milliliters) balsamic vinegar

1/8 teaspoon salt

Several grinds black pepper, to taste

Preheat the grill to medium. Remove and discard the stem ends of the zucchini and cut lengthwise into 1/4-inch slices. Place the zucchini in a plastic bag and drizzle with the olive oil and garlic. Twist the bag to seal, allowing some of the air to remain in the bag. Toss gently to coat the zucchini evenly.

Place the zucchini on the grill and grill for about 10 minutes until tender-crisp, turning two to three times. Remove the zucchini from the grill to a serving platter. Drizzle with the balsamic vinegar and sprinkle with the salt and black pepper. Serve immediately.

Yield: 4 side-dish servings

Grilled Onions
with Red Wine Vinaigrette

This recipe calls for yellow onions because they are available year-round. Early in the season, try this side dish with fresh spring torpedo-shaped onions for a delightful variation.

INGREDIENTS

4 small yellow onions

1 tablespoon (14 milliliters) olive oil

2 tablespoons (28 milliliters) extra-virgin olive oil

1 tablespoon (14 milliliters) red wine vinegar

1 tablespoon (14 milliliters) freshly squeezed lemon juice

1/2 teaspoon crushed garlic

Pinch cayenne

1 small loaf country bread, sliced

Preheat the grill to medium-high. Trim off and discard the ends of the onions and peel them. Cut the onions in half across the middle. Rub equal amounts of the olive oil over the cut sides. Place the onions, cut sides down, directly on the grill. Cover the grill and grill for about 45 minutes, turning every 10 to 12 minutes. (The onions are done when they are soft and slightly charred.)

Meanwhile, whisk together the extra-virgin olive oil, red wine vinegar, lemon juice, garlic, and cayenne in a small bowl. Place the onions on a serving platter and drizzle with the olive oil mixture. Serve immediately, passing the bread.

Yield: 4 side-dish servings

White Corn
with Chili Butter

Choose ears of corn that are fully encased by their husks, with the light-colored silk intact. You will need to tend the grill as the corn cooks because it needs to be turned frequently. The results are delicious!

INGREDIENTS

6 ears white corn, not husked

2 tablespoons (28 grams) butter

$1/2$ teaspoon crushed garlic

$1/4$ teaspoon chili powder

Pinch salt

Place the corn in a plastic bag and fill the bag with water to soak the husks for about 15 minutes.

Meanwhile, preheat the grill to high. Place the butter in a small dish and melt in the microwave oven. Add the garlic, chili powder, and salt and heat for several seconds. Set aside.

Remove the corn from the bag of water and place the corn on the grill. Turn every few minutes to evenly blacken all sides of the husks. Grill for 18 to 22 minutes. (The kernels will steam in the husks.) Remove the corn from the grill. Allow the corn to cool for a few minutes, then peel off the husks and remove the silk. Place the corn on a serving platter. Brush with the chili butter and serve immediately.

Yield: 6 side-dish servings

Grilled Red Potatoes

INGREDIENTS

6 red potatoes

2 tablespoons (28 milliliters)
  olive oil

$1/2$ teaspoon crushed garlic

$1/8$ teaspoon salt

Easy to prepare, these potatoes are good served with a skewered entrée and a dipping sauce. I enjoy them with the Dilled Yogurt and Sour Cream Sauce (page 51).

Preheat the grill to medium-high. Scrub the potatoes but do not peel them. Place the potatoes in the microwave oven and cook on high for 4 minutes, until slightly soft. Let the potatoes cool for a few minutes, then cut in half. Place the potatoes in a plastic bag and drizzle with the olive oil and garlic, then sprinkle with the salt. Twist the bag to seal, allowing some of the air to remain in the bag. Toss gently to coat the potatoes evenly. Remove the potatoes from the bag, place on the grill, and grill for 5 minutes. Turn the potatoes and continue to grill for 5 more minutes. Turn the potatoes again and grill for about 5 additional minutes on each side, until the potatoes are fork-tender and lightly browned. Serve immediately.

Yield: 6 side-dish servings

Grilled Sweet Potatoes

INGREDIENTS

4 medium red-skinned sweet
potatoes

2 tablespoons (28 milliliters)
olive oil

1/2 teaspoon granulated garlic

1/4 cup (60 grams) low-fat sour
cream

1/4 teaspoon paprika

Have you ever wondered what to do with sweet potatoes during the summertime? Grilling them is the answer! Serve them hot with grilled skewered entrées or as a finger-food appetizer while you prepare the rest of the meal.

Preheat the grill to medium-high. Scrub the sweet potatoes, but do not peel them. Slice the potatoes crosswise into 1/2-inch rounds. Place the potatoes in a plastic bag and drizzle with the olive oil, then sprinkle with the garlic. Twist the bag to seal, allowing some air to remain in the bag. Toss gently to coat the sweet potatoes evenly. Remove the potatoes from the bag and place on the grill. Grill for 10 to 12 minutes, turning frequently, until fork-tender and showing grill marks. Remove the potatoes from the grill and arrange on a large warm platter. Spoon a small amount of sour cream on top of each sweet-potato round. Sprinkle with the paprika and serve immediately.

Yield: 6 side-dish servings

Aussie Chips
with Sweet Chili Sauce

INGREDIENTS

4 russet potatoes

$^1/_4$ cup (60 milliliters) canola oil

1 teaspoon crushed garlic

$^1/_2$ teaspoon salt

$^1/_4$ cup (60 milliliters) sweet chili
  sauce

$^1/_4$ cup (60 grams) Mexican Crema
  (page 48)

My friends Candy and Al Holland's daughter, Gill, spent a semester as an exchange student in Australia. Upon her return, she raved about potatoes cooked on the grill served with a chili sauce. In Australia, "chips" are not corn chips, but are more like French fries. These chips are cooked on the grill and served with a prepared chili sauce that you can easily find in Asian markets. Kimlan makes one called Sweet Chili Sauce.

Preheat the grill to medium-high. Scrub the potatoes, but do not peel them. Cut the potatoes lengthwise into medium-thick "French-fry" wedges.

In a small bowl, whisk together the canola oil, garlic, and salt. Place the potatoes in a plastic bag and drizzle with the oil mixture. Twist the bag to seal, allowing some air to remain in the bag. Toss gently to coat the potatoes evenly.

Place the potatoes on the grill and grill for 12 to 16 minutes, turning frequently, until they are crisp on the outside and tender but moist on the inside. Transfer the potatoes to a serving platter.

Place the sweet chili sauce and Mexican Crema in small dipping bowls. Pass the potatoes, allowing diners to dip in the sauces as desired.

Yield: 8 side-dish servings

Russet Potato *Wedges*

Everyone loves baked potatoes, and these grilled wedges are a flavorful twist on that side dish. Serve with sour cream or Creamy Horseradish Sauce (page 53).

INGREDIENTS

4 medium russet potatoes

2 tablespoons (28 milliliters) olive oil

$1/2$ teaspoon paprika

$1/4$ teaspoon salt

Preheat the grill to medium-high. Scrub the potatoes but do not peel. Cut the potatoes lengthwise into wedges and place in a plastic bag. Drizzle with the olive oil and sprinkle with the paprika and salt. Twist the bag to seal, allowing some of the air to remain in the bag. Toss gently to coat the potatoes evenly.

Place the potatoes on the grill and cook for about 15 minutes, turning frequently. (The potatoes should be fork-tender but not falling apart.) Transfer the potatoes to a serving platter and serve immediately.

Yield: 6 side-dish servings

CHAPTER 6

Pizza and en Papillote Entrées

Turning your grill into a pizza oven is simple—just add a baking stone to the grill as you heat it. Then quickly transfer the pizza from a baker's peel to the baking stone on the grill and cook it— it's that easy! You may also cook the pizza on a ceramic pizza plate, preheated on the grill. The baking stone and ceramic pizza plate both produce a crisp crust and evenly cooked pizza. Be sure to sprinkle the cooking surface with cornmeal.

Prepare a fresh crust from the Basic Pizza Crust recipe on page 105 or use a commercially prepared crust. Once you've prepared the crust, the pizza comes together quickly, so be sure to have all of your ingredients chopped up, measured, and at hand, so you can place them on top of the crust and transfer it quickly to the grill.

Some of the pizza recipes I've included are on the light side, while others are more substantial. Choose salad and side dishes to accompany them depending on your diners' appetites. Pair the Pesto Pizza (page 107) or the Asparagus Pizza (page 108) with a leafy salad that is sprinkled with goat cheese for a delightful light supper. For a more hearty meal, serve the Pizza with Grilled Eggplant, Garlic, and Mozzarella (page 112) along with steamed green beans and a fresh tomato salad.

To prepare and present a fancy *en papillote* dish, you only need to master one simple technique. Tightly wrapped in kitchen parchment paper or heavy foil, the ingredients are tender, moist, and infused with flavor. The paper packets are easy to assemble and fun to serve.

How to Make and Assemble en Papillote Packets

To make kitchen parchment-paper packets, use a piece of parchment about 15-x-18 inches for each serving. Fold each piece of parchment in half and crease it to create 7-x-12-inch rectangles. Use scissors to cut each rectangle into a half-heart shape. Open out the hearts and distribute equal amounts of the ingredients, positioning them near the center of each crease. Add any spices or liquids to each packet. Close the heart so that the edges of the paper meet. Beginning at the round end, fold over about 1/2 inch of the paper and crease sharply. Work your way around the shape of the heart, folding in the edges and creasing sharply in overlapping pleats. Twist the pointy end to seal everything tightly in the packet. Repeat this process with the remaining packets.

For heavy-duty foil packets, use a 12-x-18-inch piece of foil for each packet. Place the foil on a work surface, creasing it lengthwise in the center. Mound the ingredients on one side of the crease. Add any spices or liquids to each packet. Fold the other section of the foil over the ingredients. Crimp the side sections to seal. You can do a fancy presentation by forming the remaining narrow end into a "swan's neck" by twisting it and forming an "S" shape. Crimp the bottom to form a "tail."

When you're ready to cook, place the packets in a single layer on a baking stone and grill for about 15 minutes. I like to remove the packets from the grill directly to the serving plate and allow the diners to open their packets, releasing the aromas that have built up inside. The Curried Cauliflower and Carrots *en Papillote* (page 117) and the Asparagus, Shiitake Mushrooms and Tofu *en Papillote* (page 119) are particularly aromatic.

The *en papillote* packets may be prepared ahead of time and refrigerated until you are ready to put them on the grill. Add a couple of minutes to the cooking time because the ingredients will be cold. These recipes are easy to double, so they are wonderful to prepare for a dinner party.

Basic Pizza Crust

INGREDIENTS

¹/₄ ounce (7 grams) active dry
   yeast (1 envelope)

1 ¹/₂ cups (355 milliliters) lukewarm water (105° to 115°F)

2 tablespoons (28 milliliters) plus
   ¹/₂ teaspoon olive oil

¹/₂ teaspoon salt

3 ¹/₂ to 4 cups (440 to 500 grams)
   unbleached white flour

Use bread flour or unbleached white flour. The flour measure is given as a range because the exact amount of flour will vary depending on the day's humidity and other weather conditions. The temperature of the water to start the yeast is important—if it's too hot, it will kill the yeast; if it's too cold, the yeast will not be activated. Use an instant-read thermometer to make sure the water temperature is in the 105° to 115°F range.

Place the yeast in a large warm bowl and add the lukewarm water. Stir the mixture with a wooden spoon to dissolve the yeast, then set aside in a warm place until creamy in appearance, about 15 minutes. Stir in 2 tablespoons of the olive oil and the salt, and then add 2 cups of the flour. Stir to incorporate, using a large wooden spoon. (The mixture will be very sticky at this point.) Add 1 more cup of the flour and continue to stir until the dough begins to form a ball. Turn the dough out onto a lightly floured work surface and knead the dough until it is soft and smooth, about 10 minutes, adding the remaining ¹/₂ cup flour as needed, a bit at a time, until the dough

continued on next page >

is no longer sticky. If necessary, add up to $^1/_2$ cup more flour, a tablespoon at a time. (Too much flour will result in a dry dough that will produce a slightly tough crust.)

Lightly oil a large bowl with the remaining $^1/_2$ teaspoon oil. Place the dough ball in the oiled bowl, turn it to coat the entire surface with oil, and cover the bowl with a clean dish towel. Place the bowl in a warm, draft-free place for the dough to rise until doubled in volume, about $1^1/_2$ hours.

After the dough has risen, punch it down with your fist to press out most of the air.

Place the dough on a lightly floured work surface and divide it into 2 balls of equal size. Working with 1 ball at a time, flatten the dough with your hands into a circle about 4 inches in diameter and 1 inch thick. Begin working from the center, pressing the dough outward with the heels of your hands. (If the dough sticks to your hands, sprinkle it lightly with flour.) Push the dough into a 12-inch round that is slightly thicker at the edges. (You can also use a rolling pin to press the dough into a 12-inch round.)

If you are only making one pizza, wrap the remaining dough ball tightly and freeze it for up to 3 months. Thaw the dough at room temperature for a few hours before rolling out as directed above. Proceed with the instructions for the individual recipes.

Yield: two 12-inch pizza crusts

Pesto Pizza

INGREDIENTS

1 pizza crust (12 inches/
    30 centimeters in diameter)
2 tablespoons (17 grams)
    cornmeal
$^1/_4$ cup (60 grams) prepared
    marinara sauce
1 cup (150 grams) coarsely
    grated mozzarella cheese
1 tablespoon (14 milliliters)
    olive oil
$^3/_4$ cup (200 grams) Basil
    Pesto (page 23)

One of the joys of having a summer garden is growing fresh basil to turn into pesto! It only takes a couple of plants to produce abundant harvests—and you can grow interesting varieties like lemon basil that can be hard to find at the grocery. However, if you don't have access to fresh basil, you may use commercially prepared pesto in this recipe. This pizza is heaven on a warm summer day.

Prepare the Basic Pizza Crust (page 105) or use a commercially prepared crust. Place a baking stone or ceramic pizza plate on the grill and preheat the grill to high.

Place the uncooked crust on a baker's peel or rimless baking sheet that is well dusted with the cornmeal. Spread the marinara sauce evenly over the uncooked crust, leaving a 1-inch rim. Sprinkle the mozzarella cheese evenly over the sauce. Brush the rim of the uncooked crust with the olive oil.

Transfer the pizza to the baking stone on the grill. Bake for 15 to 20 minutes, until the crust is crisp and the cheese has melted. Remove the pizza from the grill and drizzle with the Basil Pesto. Cut the pizza into 8 slices and serve immediately.

Yield: 2 main-dish servings or 4 side-dish servings

Asparagus Pizza

This pizza is light and flavorful. Serve it for dinner with a big salad or as part of a luncheon party.

INGREDIENTS

1 bulb garlic

2 1/4 teaspoons olive oil

1 pizza crust (12 inches/
   30 centimeters in diameter)

8 medium-thick stalks asparagus

2 tablespoons (17 grams) cornmeal

1 cup (130 grams) coarsely grated
   Fontina cheese

1/4 cup (25 grams) chopped
   kalamata olives

1/2 cup (55 grams) crumbled soft
   goat cheese

Preheat the grill to medium. Rub the papery skin from the garlic, but do not break into individual cloves. Cut about 1/2-inch off the pointed top end of the bulb and rub the surface with 1/4 teaspoon of the olive oil. Place the garlic bulb, cut side up, in a covered clay or glass baking dish and place on the grill. (You could wrap the garlic in foil. Then place the foil packet on a baking stone or on baking bricks so the garlic cooks but does not burn on the bottom.) Grill for about 45 minutes. When the garlic feels very soft when gently squeezed, remove from the grill and uncover to cool. When the garlic is cool enough to handle, squeeze the garlic from the individual cloves into a small bowl and set aside.

Prepare the Basic Pizza Crust (page 105) or use a commercially prepared crust.

Snap off and discard the tough ends from the asparagus and cut the stems at a slant into 1-inch pieces. Place the asparagus in a plastic bag and drizzle with 1 teaspoon of the olive oil. Twist the bag to seal, allowing some of the air to remain in the bag. Toss gently to coat the asparagus evenly. Remove the asparagus from the bag. Place a grill basket on the grill and evenly distribute the asparagus in the basket. Grill for 5 to 6 minutes, turning frequently. Remove the asparagus and grill basket, and set aside. Place the baking stone or ceramic pizza plate on the grill and increase the grill temperature to high.

Place the uncooked crust on a baker's peel or rimless baking sheet that is well dusted with the cornmeal. Use a rubber spatula to spread the garlic over the crust. Evenly sprinkle the Fontina cheese over the crust, leaving a 1-inch rim. Top with the asparagus and kalamata olives. Crumble the goat cheese over the pizza. Brush the rim of the crust with the remaining 1 teaspoon olive oil.

Transfer the pizza to the baking stone or ceramic pizza plate on the grill. Bake for 15 to 20 minutes, until the crust is crisp and the cheese has melted. Remove from the grill and cut into 8 slices. Serve immediately.

Yield: 4 main-dish servings

Asparagus and Mushroom Pizza
with Mustard, Dill, Mozzarella, and Feta

INGREDIENTS

1 pizza crust (12 inches/
30 centimeters in diameter)

2 tablespoons (17 grams)
cornmeal

1 pound (455 grams) asparagus

1/2 pound (225 grams) button
mushrooms, sliced

3 cloves garlic, minced

1/8 teaspoon salt

Several grinds black pepper,
to taste

2 tablespoons (30 grams) whole
grain mustard

1/3 cup (40 grams) thinly sliced
red onion

4 ounces (115 grams) grated
mozzarella cheese

1 ounce (28 grams) crumbled feta
cheese

3 teaspoons minced fresh dill

1/4 teaspoon paprika

Asparagus is a springtime treat, and this innovative pizza is just one more way to enjoy this succulent vegetable.

Prepare the Basic Pizza Crust (page 105) or use a commercially prepared crust. Place a baking stone or ceramic pizza plate on the grill and preheat the grill to high. Place the uncooked crust on a baker's peel or rimless baking sheet that is well dusted with the cornmeal. Set aside.

Rinse the asparagus. Break off and discard the tough ends. Slice the asparagus at a slant into 1-inch pieces. Place the asparagus in a skillet on the stovetop with the mushrooms, garlic, salt, black pepper, and 2 tablespoons (28 milliliters) water. Cover and cook over medium heat for 5 minutes, then remove the lid and continue to cook for about 5 minutes, stirring frequently. (Most of the liquid should have evaporated.)

Meanwhile, use a rubber spatula to spread the mustard over the pizza crust, leaving a 1-inch rim around the outside. Use a slotted spoon to transfer the asparagus mixture to the pizza, spreading it out evenly and leaving a 1-inch rim around the outer edge. Distribute the onion slices evenly over the asparagus mixture, and then top with the mozzarella cheese. Sprinkle the feta cheese and dill over the mozzarella cheese, and then dust with the paprika.

Transfer the pizza to the baking stone or ceramic pizza plate on the grill. Bake for 15 to 20 minutes, until the crust is crisp and the cheese has softened and browned a bit. Remove the pizza from the grill and cut into 8 wedges. Serve immediately.

Yield: 4 main-dish servings

Pizza with Garlic Tomato Sauce, Ricotta, and Fresh Greens

INGREDIENTS

1 pizza crust (12 inches/
    30 centimeters in diameter)

2 tablespoons (17 grams)
    cornmeal

3 pear tomatoes

2 tablespoons (35 grams)
    tomato paste

2 cloves garlic, minced

6 teaspoons finely grated
    Parmesan cheese

$1/4$ cup (25 grams) chopped
    kalamata olives

$1/2$ cup (125 grams) part-skim
    ricotta cheese

2 tablespoons (30 grams)
    low-fat sour cream

1 teaspoon dried oregano

1 tablespoon (14 milliliters)
    olive oil

1 teaspoon lemon juice

$1/8$ teaspoon salt

Several grinds black pepper, to
    taste

$1 1/2$ cups (40 grams) mixed baby
    salad greens

This pizza is salad and entrée all in one! Prepare it for a lovely lunch or light supper.

Prepare the Basic Pizza Crust (page 105) or use a commercially prepared crust. Place a baking stone or ceramic pizza plate on the grill and preheat the grill to high. Place the uncooked crust on a baker's peel or rimless baking sheet that is well dusted with the cornmeal.

Without peeling them, cut the tomatoes into quarters and place them in a blender. Add the tomato paste and garlic, then puree until smooth and set aside.

Sprinkle the Parmesan cheese evenly over the crust, then evenly top with the pureed tomatoes, leaving a 1-inch border free of sauce. Distribute the kalamata olives on top of the sauce.

In a bowl, combine the ricotta cheese, sour cream, and $1/2$ teaspoon of the oregano. Place 8 heaping tablespoons of the mixture on the pizza, within the ring of sauce and extending toward its outer edge. Crumble the remaining $1/2$ teaspoon oregano over the pizza. Transfer the pizza to the baking stone or ceramic pizza plate on the grill. Bake for 15 to 20 minutes, until the crust is crisp and the cheese has softened and browned a bit.

Meanwhile, in a small bowl, whisk together the olive oil, lemon juice, salt, and black pepper. Place the greens in a bowl and drizzle with the dressing. Remove the pizza from the grill and cut into 8 wedges. Mound the greens in the center of the pizza and serve immediately.

Yield: 4 main-dish servings

Pizza with Grilled Eggplant, Garlic, and Mozzarella

INGREDIENTS

1 pizza crust (12 inches/
   30 centimeters in diameter)

1 bulb garlic

2 tablespoons (28 milliliters)
   plus 1 1/4 teaspoons olive oil

1 medium eggplant

2 tablespoons (17 grams)
   cornmeal

1/4 cup (60 milliliters) Tomato
   Coulis (page 24)

6 ounces (170 grams) grated
   mozzarella cheese

1/4 teaspoon dried oregano

1/8 teaspoons salt

Several grinds black pepper,
   to taste

This pizza is the perfect summer entrée when the garden yields fresh, sweet tomatoes and tender eggplant. Prepare the Tomato Coulis in advance so these ingredients are ready when you begin to prepare the pizza.

Prepare the Basic Pizza Crust (page 105) or use a commercially prepared crust. Preheat the grill to medium. Rub the papery skin from the garlic, but do not break into individual cloves. Cut about 1/2 inch off the pointed top end of the bulb and rub the cut surface with 1/4 teaspoon of the olive oil. Place the garlic bulb, cut side up, in a covered clay or glass baking dish and place on the grill. (You can wrap it in foil. Then place the foil packet on a baking stone or on baking bricks so the garlic cooks but does not burn on the bottom.) Grill for about 45 minutes. When the garlic feels very soft when gently squeezed, remove from the grill and uncover to cool.

Remove and discard the stem of the eggplant, but do not peel. Cut the eggplant lengthwise into 1/4-inch slices. Brush one side of the eggplant slices with 1 tablespoon of the olive oil and place the eggplant oiled sides down on the grill. Grill for 4 to 6 minutes. Brush the top side of the eggplant with 1 tablespoon of the oil and turn. Continue to grill for 4 to 6 minutes. Remove from the grill and set aside.

Place a baking stone or ceramic pizza plate on the grill and increase the grill temperature to high.

Place the uncooked pizza crust on a baker's peel or a rimless baking sheet that is well dusted with the cornmeal. Press the garlic from the skins into a small bowl and spread evenly over the crust. Spread the Tomato Coulis over the garlic on the pizza crust. Distribute half of the mozzarella cheese evenly over the tomato sauce and then arrange the eggplant slices evenly over that in a fan pattern. Distribute the remaining cheese over the eggplant. Drizzle the outer edge of the pizza with the remaining teaspoon of olive oil. Sprinkle the pizza with the oregano, salt, and black pepper.

Transfer the pizza to the baking stone on the grill. Bake for 15 to 20 minutes, until the crust is crisp and the cheese is melted. Remove the pizza from the grill and cut into 8 wedges. Serve immediately.

Pizza with Zucchini,
Artichokes, and Feta Cheese

Although inspired by the flavors common to the Mediterranean, this pizza is easy to prepare in your own backyard, no matter where that may be.

INGREDIENTS

1 pizza crust (12 inches/
   30 centimeters in diameter)

2 tablespoons (17 grams)
   cornmeal

14 ounces (400 grams) canned
   water-packed artichoke hearts

1 medium zucchini

2 ounces (55 grams) thinly sliced
   Provolone cheese

1/2 small red onion, thinly sliced

6 teaspoons minced fresh oregano

2 ounces (55 grams) crumbled
   feta cheese

Several grinds black pepper,
   to taste

Prepare the Basic Pizza Crust (page 105) or use a commercially prepared crust. Place a baking stone or ceramic pizza plate on the grill and preheat the grill to high. Place the uncooked crust on a baker's peel or rimless baking sheet that is well dusted with the cornmeal.

Drain the artichoke hearts and coarsely chop them. Remove and discard the ends of the zucchini and cut it into very thin oblong slices. Distribute the Provolone slices so that they cover most of the pizza crust, leaving a 1-inch border. Arrange the onion over the top of the Provolone cheese, then place the zucchini and artichoke hearts on top of the onion. Distribute the oregano and the feta cheese over the top and grind on the black pepper.

Transfer the pizza to the baking stone or ceramic pizza plate on the grill. Bake for 15 to 20 minutes, until the crust is crisp and the cheese has melted. Cut into 8 wedges and serve immediately.

Yield: 4 main-dish servings

Grilled Pepper and Chard Pizza
with Cumin, Jalapeños, and Cilantro

INGREDIENTS

1 pizza crust (12 inches/
   30 centimeters in diameter)

1 large red bell pepper

1 pound (455 grams) Swiss chard

1 tablespoon (14 milliliters) olive oil

1 small yellow onion, diced

6 cloves garlic, minced

1 1/2 teaspoons cumin seed

Scant 1/8 teaspoon salt

2 tablespoons (17 grams) cornmeal

2 ounces (55 grams) grated
   Monterey Jack cheese

1/4 cup (25 grams) finely grated
   Parmesan cheese

3 teaspoons minced pickled
   jalapeño chiles

6 teaspoons minced fresh cilantro

A spicy delight, this dish combines some classic Tex-Mex flavors on a pizza crust.

Prepare the Basic Pizza Crust (page 105) or use a commercially prepared one. Preheat the grill to high. Place the bell pepper directly on the grill and grill for 10 to 15 minutes, turning frequently. (The skin will be charred black.) Transfer the pepper to a plastic or paper bag, close the bag, and set aside for 15 minutes. When the pepper is cool enough to handle, peel off the skin and discard the stem, seeds, and white membrane. Thinly slice the pepper and set aside.

Wash the chard leaves, but do not dry them. Thinly slice the stems and coarsely chop the leaves; set the stems and leaves aside separately.

Heat the olive oil in a skillet over medium heat. Add the onion, garlic, cumin, and salt and sauté for a moment, then stir in the chard stems and salt. Sauté for 5 minutes, then mound the greens on top, cover tightly, and cook an additional 5 minutes. (The greens should be wilted.) Stir to combine them with the other ingredients in the pan. Continue to cook for a minute or two, stirring constantly, until all the liquid has evaporated. Remove from the heat.

Place a baking stone or ceramic pizza plate on the grill.

Place the uncooked crust on a baker's peel or rimless baking sheet that is well dusted with the cornmeal. Distribute the cooked greens evenly over the pizza crust and arrange the pepper slices on top of them in a pretty pattern.

In a small bowl, toss together the Monterey Jack cheese, Parmesan cheese, jalapeño chiles, and cilantro. Distribute evenly over the pizza. Transfer the pizza to the baking stone or ceramic pizza plate on the grill. Bake for 15 to 20 minutes, until the crust is crisp and the cheese has melted. Remove from the grill and cut into 8 slices. Serve immediately.

Yield: 4 main-dish servings

Individual Pizzas
with Tomatoes, Feta, and Kalamata Olives

INGREDIENTS

2 medium plum tomatoes, diced

1/4 cup (10 grams) chopped fresh
basil

2 tablespoons (15 grams) capers,
drained

Several grinds black pepper, to
taste

4 whole-wheat pita breads or
Middle Eastern flat breads

1/4 cup (60 milliliters) olive oil

1/2 cup (50 grams) chopped
kalamata olives

4 green onions, diced

6 ounces (170 grams) crumbled
feta

This is a fabulous quick summer dinner to prepare. The individual pizzas can be customized to each diner's taste, or all prepared the same way. As the pizzas grill, the feta cheese does not melt, but it becomes soft as all of the ingredients heat through.

Place the tomatoes in a bowl and add the basil, capers, and black pepper. Set aside.

Preheat the grill to medium. Brush one side of each pita bread or flat bread with some of the olive oil and place on the grill, oiled sides down, for 1 to 2 minutes. Remove the pitas from the grill to a baker's peel or rimless baking sheet and brush the other sides with olive oil. Turn the pitas over and top the grilled sides with equal amounts of the tomato mixture, olives, green onions, and feta cheese.

Place the pitas back on the grill, oiled sides down, and grill for 2 to 3 minutes. Remove from the grill and cut into wedges. Serve immediately.

Yield: 4 main-dish servings

Curried Cauliflower
and Carrots en Papillote

INGREDIENTS

2 cups (300 grams) cauliflower florets

2 cups (260 grams) diced carrots

4 large cloves garlic, peeled and sliced

1/4 cup (55 grams) unsalted butter, melted

2 tablespoons (28 milliliters) cooking sherry

1 teaspoon curry powder

1/4 teaspoon salt

1 cup (175 grams) uncooked orzo

1/4 cup (4 grams) minced fresh cilantro

4 lime wedges

This is a fancy and flavorful way to serve cauliflower and carrots. The accent of the cilantro and lime finishes the dish.

Place a baking stone on the grill and preheat the grill to medium-high before you are ready to cook the packets. (See "How to Make and Assemble *en Papillote* Packets" on page 104 for instructions on how to use this cooking technique.)

Distribute the cauliflower, carrots, and garlic evenly among four 12-x-18-inch pieces of kitchen parchment paper or heavy-duty foil, positioning them near the center of each crease. Set aside.

Melt the butter in a small pan and add the sherry, curry powder, and salt. Drizzle an equal amount over each mound of vegetables.

Close the kitchen parchment or heavy-duty foil packets. When ready to cook, place the packets in a single layer on the baking stone and bake for about 15 minutes.

Meanwhile, heat water in a medium-size saucepan on the stove-top over high heat for the orzo. When the water is boiling, add the orzo. Reduce the heat to medium-high and cook for about 15 minutes. Drain the orzo into a colander.

Transfer the packets to warmed serving plates. Have each diner pinch and tear the paper to release the aromatic steam. The contents may then be lifted out onto the plates and the papers removed from the table. Pass the cooked orzo. Have diners sprinkle the cilantro and squeeze the lime juice over the dish as desired.

Yield: 4 main-dish servings

Potatoes, Mushrooms, and Shallots en Papillote

Serve this elegantly presented but comforting dish with cheese and crusty bread for a lovely meal.

INGREDIENTS

1 1/2 pounds (700 grams) red potatoes, diced

1 pound (455 grams) button mushrooms, sliced

4 shallots, peeled and sliced

1/4 cup (55 grams) butter, melted

1/4 cup (60 milliliters) cooking sherry

2 teaspoons horseradish

2 teaspoons dried oregano

1/2 teaspoon salt

Several grinds black pepper, to taste

2 pounds (1 kilogram) fresh spinach

1 tablespoon (14 milliliters) white vinegar

6 large eggs

Place a baking stone on the grill and preheat the grill to medium-high before you are ready to cook the packets. (See "How to Make and Assemble *en Papillote* Packets" on page 104 for instructions on how to use this cooking technique.)

Distribute the potatoes, mushrooms, and shallots evenly among six 12-x-18-inch pieces of kitchen parchment paper or heavy-duty foil, positioning them near the center of each crease.

Mix the butter, sherry, horseradish, oregano, salt, and black pepper together in a small bowl or measuring cup. Pour equal amounts of the butter mixture over the individual vegetable packets.

Close the kitchen parchment or heavy-duty foil packets. When ready to cook, place the packets in a single layer on the baking stone and bake for 15 to 20 minutes.

Meanwhile, remove the stems from the spinach and place the leaves in a colander. Rinse well to remove any dirt. Place the wet spinach in a large stockpot on the stovetop over medium-high heat, cover, and steam for 5 minutes. Transfer the spinach to a colander to drain. Return the spinach to the stockpot, cover, and keep warm.

Place a shallow pan on the stovetop and fill with water. Cover and bring to a boil. Add the vinegar and reduce the heat to a strong simmer. Stir the water in a circular motion and carefully add each egg. (Add each egg directly from the cracked shell or break an egg into a saucer and slip it gently from the saucer into the water.) As the eggs cook, use a large spoon to dip some water from around the sides of the eggs and pour it over them to cook the tops. When a film forms over the yolks and the whites are firm, the eggs are cooked. (This takes about 5 minutes.)

Transfer the packets to warmed serving plates. Place equal amounts of spinach on each plate and top with a poached egg. Have each diner pinch and tear the paper to release the aromatic steam. The contents may then be lifted out onto the plates and the papers removed from the table.

Yield: 6 main-dish servings

Asparagus, Shiitake Mushrooms, and Tofu en Papillote

INGREDIENTS

14 ounces (400 grams) extra-firm
tofu

1 pound (455 grams) asparagus

1/2 pound (225 grams) fresh
shiitake mushrooms

1/3 cup (75 milliliters)
unsweetened coconut milk

3 tablespoons (3 grams) minced
cilantro

1 teaspoon freshly squeezed
lemon juice

2 cloves garlic, minced

1 teaspoon soy sauce

1 teaspoon grated fresh ginger

Pinch cayenne pepper

2 to 3 cups (390 to 585 grams)
cooked brown basmati rice

The Thai seasonings create the perfect balance of sweet and pungent flavors in this entrée. Prepare the rice ahead of time and have it steaming hot when ready to serve.

Place a baking stone on the grill and preheat the grill to medium-high before you are ready to cook the packets. (See "How to Make and Assemble *en Papillote* Packets" on page 112 for instructions on how to use this cooking technique.)

Rinse the tofu and cut it in half through the middle, then into 12 strips. Wash the asparagus and snap off and discard the tough ends. Cut the asparagus at a slant into 1-inch pieces. Remove and discard the stem ends from the mushrooms and slice the caps. Set aside.

In a small bowl, stir together the coconut milk, cilantro, lemon juice, garlic, soy sauce, ginger, and cayenne pepper.

Distribute the asparagus spears lengthwise among four 12-x-18-inch pieces of cooking parchment paper or heavy-duty foil, positioning them near the center of each crease. Top with equal amounts of the mushrooms. Place an equal number of tofu strips on top of the asparagus. Pour the sauce evenly over the tofu.

Close the kitchen parchment or heavy-duty foil packets. When ready to cook, place the packets in a single layer on the baking stone and bake for about 15 minutes.

Transfer the packets to warmed serving plates. Have each diner pinch and tear the paper to release the aromatic steam. The contents may then be lifted out onto the plates and the papers removed from the table. Pass the cooked basmati rice.

Yield: 4 main-dish servings

Summer Squashes
en Papillote with Tex-Mex Seasonings

INGREDIENTS

I teaspoon cumin seed

I teaspoon chili powder

$^1/_2$ teaspoon granulated garlic

$^1/_8$ teaspoon salt

Several grinds black pepper,
   to taste

I pound (455 grams) summer
   squashes, cubed or whole
   if small

I red bell pepper, thinly sliced

I small yellow onion, diced

6 teaspoons minced fresh cilantro

4 teaspoons dry white wine

2 teaspoons olive oil

2 tablespoons (20 grams) raw,
   unsalted pumpkin seeds

2 cups (390 grams) cooked
   brown rice

2 cups (345 grams) cooked
   black beans

You may use any type of summer squash for this dish, but a colorful variety is most pleasing to the eye. If you can find bite-size baby squashes, you can cook them whole for a stunning effect. Cook the rice and black beans before you are ready to serve the packets and serve them steaming hot. Pass Pear and Avocado Salsa (page 39), if you wish, for a perfect accompaniment.

Place a baking stone on the grill and preheat the grill to medium-high before you are ready to cook the packets. (See "How to Make and Assemble *en Papillote* Packets" on page 104 for instructions on how to use this cooking technique.)

Use a mortar and pestle or spice grinder to crush the cumin seed.

In a small bowl, stir together the cumin seed, chili powder, garlic, salt, and black pepper. Set aside.

Distribute the squash, bell pepper, and onion evenly among four 12-x-18-inch pieces of cooking parchment paper or heavy-duty foil, positioning them near the center of each crease. Sprinkle equal amounts of the spice mixture and cilantro over the vegetables. Drizzle 1 teaspoon of the wine and $^1/_2$ teaspoon of the olive oil over each packet.

Close the kitchen parchment or heavy-duty foil packets. When ready to cook, place the packets in a single layer on the baking stone and bake for about 15 minutes.

Meanwhile, place the pumpkin seeds in a single layer in a heavy, dry skillet on the stovetop over medium heat. Shake or stir the seeds frequently. When they begin to pop, keep the seeds moving. (You want them to pop but not get too brown.) Remove the pumpkin seeds from the pan, let them cool a bit, and mince them. Set the pumpkin seeds aside in a small serving dish.

Transfer the packets to warmed serving plates. Have each diner pinch and tear the paper to release the aromatic steam. The contents may then be lifted out onto the plates and the papers removed from the table. Pass the cooked brown rice, black beans, and pumpkin seeds.

Yield: 4 main-dish servings

Broccoli and Mushrooms
en Papillote with Paprika, Feta, and Dill Seed

INGREDIENTS

1 teaspoon paprika

^{1}/$_2$ teaspoon crushed dill seed

Pinch salt

Several grinds black pepper,
   to taste

1^1/$_4$ pounds (570 grams) broccoli

^{1}/$_4$ pound (115 grams) button
   mushrooms

^{1}/$_2$ red onion, thinly sliced

1/4 cup (60 milliliters) dark beer

3 ounces (85 grams) crumbled
   feta cheese

4 lemon wedges

2 to 3 cups (390 to 585 grams)
   cooked brown basmati rice

This delectable dish features the distinctive flavors of Eastern Europe. The ingredients are available year-round, so enjoy this dish any time you want to fire up the grill. Have the rice cooked and steaming hot when you are ready to serve.

Place a baking stone on the grill and preheat the grill to medium-high before you are ready to cook the packets. See "How to Make and Assemble *en Papillote* Packets" on page 104 for instructions on how to use this cooking technique.)

In a small bowl, combine the paprika, dill seed, salt, and black pepper. Cut off and discard the tough stem ends of the broccoli and peel the remaining stalks if they are particularly thick-skinned. Cut the broccoli lengthwise into even-size spears. Bush or wipe loose dirt particles from the mushrooms and quarter them.

Distribute the broccoli spears evenly among four 12-x-18-inch pieces of cooking parchment paper or heavy-duty foil, positioning them near the center of each crease. Add one-quarter of the mushrooms and onion to each packet, arranging loosely on top of the broccoli. Sprinkle equal amounts of the paprika mixture over the vegetables and pour equal amounts of the beer over each portion. Top with equal amounts of feta cheese. Close the kitchen parchment or heavy-duty foil packets.

When ready to cook, place the packets in a single layer on the baking stone and bake for about 15 minutes. Transfer the packets to warmed serving plates. Have each diner pinch and tear the paper to release the aromatic steam. The contents may then be lifted out onto the plates and the papers removed from the table. Serve with the lemon and pass the cooked basmati rice.

Yield: 4 main-dish servings

Summer Squash Stuffed
with Sweet Pepper Couscous en Papillote

INGREDIENTS

1 cup (175 grams) uncooked couscous

1 cup (235 milliliters) white wine

1/4 cup (60 milliliters) freshly squeezed lemon juice

3 teaspoons granulated garlic

2 small yellow crookneck squashes

4 small zucchini

2 scallop squashes

1/4 cup (25 grams) finely diced red bell pepper

1/4 cup (25 grams) finely diced yellow bell pepper

1/4 cup (25 grams) finely diced green bell pepper

1 jalapeño chile, seeded and minced

1 large egg, beaten

1 tablespoon (14 milliliters) extra-virgin olive oil

1 1/2 ounces (45 grams) manchego cheese, grated

This en papillote *dish is best prepared wrapped in one large foil packet. All of the flavors steam together as they cook—the resulting dish is delicious. Manchego cheese is a semi-hard sheep-milk cheese from Spain.*

Place the couscous in a bowl and add 1/2 cup of the wine and the lemon juice and garlic. Stir to combine and set aside for 5 to 10 minutes.

Preheat the grill to medium-high. Cut the crookneck squashes, zucchini, and scallop squashes in half lengthwise and use a spoon or melon baller to scoop out the centers, being careful to leave at least a 1/4-inch-thick shell. Place 1/2 cup of the pulp in a bowl and add the bell peppers and jalapeño chile. Stir to combine. Add the couscous along with the egg and olive oil. Stir to incorporate. Stuff each squash cavity with the couscous filling and place on a large sheet of foil. Top with the manchego cheese.

Crimp the edges of the packet and pour the remaining 1/2 cup of wine into the packet, then fold over the top and sides to seal. Place the packet on the grill and cook for 15 to 18 minutes. Remove the packet from the grill and place on a large platter or on individual serving plates and serve immediately.

Yield: 6 main-dish servings

CHAPTER 7

Pasta, Grain, and Polenta Dishes

In this chapter, it is not necessarily the pasta, grain, or polenta that is grilled, but the components that go into the dish are, yielding a delicious meal. Several recipes feature grilled polenta—a fabulous way to serve this humble cornmeal—but most use the pasta or grain as the base to showcase the grilled items. It is critical, however, to master the art of preparing perfectly cooked pasta, rice, and polenta.

Every excellent pasta dish begins with excellent pasta. Italian households typically use dried pasta made of semolina flour and water, and this variety is preferred for most recipes in this chapter. That said, when preparing an Asian-themed dish, use soba noodles, made from buckwheat flour.

Cooking pasta is simple—bring a large pot of water to a boil on the stovetop and add the pasta. The caveat is placing the proper amount of water in the pot and determining the cooking time. Plenty of water, 6 to 8 quarts per pound of pasta, will prevent the pasta from sticking to the pot. Bring the water to a strong, rolling boil, then add the pasta and stir it vigorously a few times while it is cooking.

Pasta should be cooked *al dente*. The Italian phrase literally means "to the tooth," suggesting that the tooth should meet a little resistance when biting into the pasta. Recommended cooking times vary and are usually listed on the package. Set your timer for a couple of minutes less than the recommended time, and when the timer goes off, remove a noodle from the pot. If it is undercooked, it will stick to your teeth when you bite into it. Continue to cook, testing again every minute or so, until the pasta is tender but not mushy. This is the sought-after al dente stage. As you master cooking pasta, you will be able to look at it and tell when it is done! Drain the al dente pasta immediately in a large, footed colander. Shake the colander to remove excess water, but do not rinse the pasta.

Rice is best prepared in a pot that has a tight-fitting lid and is the appropriate size for the amount of rice that you are cooking. Add the rice to rapidly boiling water, then cover and cook it over very low heat. Whole grain rice, such as brown rice, takes the longest to cook, so put it on at least 45 minutes before you plan to serve the meal. Basmati rice is a fragrant variety from India and a favorite of mine. You will find brown and white basmati, both of which should be rinsed right before cooking. This removes some of the starch and yields fluffy rice. Brown basmati cooks in about 35 minutes, while the white basmati takes only about 20 minutes.

Risotto dishes use a unique, oval, short-grained rice—usually Fino Arborio—that releases its starch gradually during the cooking process to create a creamy texture. Do not rinse Arborio rice before cooking because you do not want to wash away any of the surface starches. Cook risotto in an open pot, adding small amounts of liquid as it cooks. To prevent sticking or scorching, stir risotto almost constantly as it absorbs each addition of liquid. If risotto sticks despite stirring, reduce the heat slightly. Since risotto requires vigilant stirring, you may want to enlist the help of a friend or family member. If the recommended amount of liquid is absorbed before the rice is tender, add more hot stock or water, $1/2$ cup at a time, until the rice is tender and the consistency for the risotto is creamy, not sticky.

The last grain showcased in this chapter is polenta. Basically cornmeal mush elevated to gastronomic heights by innovative seasonings and toppings, polenta is served either creamy and soft or firm. Soft polenta is always served hot, while the firm style is shaped in a loaf and grilled.

Polenta is best cooked in a heavy-bottomed saucepan on the stovetop. Essential tools include a whisk for adding the polenta to the boiling water and a long-handled wooden spoon for stirring as the polenta thickens. To avoid lumps in the finished dish, add the polenta to the hot water gradually over the course of a minute or two, pouring in a slow, steady stream. Whisk continuously while you are adding it to the water. For polenta that is to be served creamy and soft, prepare it to come off the stove right before serving. For firm, grilled polenta such as Grilled Polenta with Tomato Coulis (page 147), prepare the polenta in advance and allow it to set up in a loaf pan for several hours before slicing and grilling it.

The grilled ingredients of each of these recipes play the starring role in the dish. Some dishes are seasonal, like the Pasta with Grilled Asparagus and Onions (page 127), Risotto with Grilled Corn and Red Peppers (page 144), and Vermicelli with Grilled Tomato Sauce (page 128). Other recipes call for ingredients that are more seasonless. Enjoy Grilled Portobello Mushrooms with Couscous and Gruyère Cheese (page 136) or Pistachio-Encrusted Tofu with Basmati Rice (page 143) any time of the year.

Pasta with Grilled Asparagus
and Onions

INGREDIENTS

1/3 cup (75 milliliters) extra-virgin
   olive oil

3 tablespoons (45 milliliters)
   freshly squeezed lemon juice

3 teaspoons minced fresh
   tarragon

3 teaspoons minced fresh flat-leaf
   parsley

I tablespoon (15 grams) Dijon
   mustard

1/2 teaspoon salt

Several grinds fresh black pepper,
   to taste

3 red torpedo-shaped onions

2 tablespoons (28 milliliters)
   olive oil

2 pounds (1 kilogram) fresh
   asparagus

Pinch salt

I pound (455 grams) rotini pasta

Grated parmesan cheese
   (optional)

I like this pasta dish in the spring, when you can purchase fresh onions and asparagus at the farmers' market. Choose the thickest asparagus stalks you can because they are succulent and will produce the best results. I like a rotini or fusilli pasta for this dish. This dish is best made ahead of time and served at room temperature.

Prepare the dressing by whisking together the extra-virgin olive oil, lemon juice, tarragon, parsley, mustard, 1/2 teaspoon salt, and black pepper in a small bowl. Set aside.

Preheat the grill to medium. Trim and discard the green tops and root ends from the onions and peel them. Slice them lengthwise, brush with some of the olive oil, and set aside.

Wash the asparagus carefully to remove any traces of soil. Snap off the tough ends. Place the asparagus in a plastic bag and drizzle with the remaining olive oil. Twist the bag to seal, allowing some of the air to remain in the bag. Toss gently to coat the asparagus evenly.

Place the onions on the grill. Grill the onions for 15 to 18 minutes until they are soft, but not falling apart, turning twice. Remove the asparagus from the bag, place on a grill grate, and transfer to the grill. Grill the asparagus for 8 to 10 minutes, sprinkling with the pinch of salt and turning frequently so the stalks cook but do not burn. Grill just until al dente; they will be slightly charred. Remove the onions and asparagus from the grill and set aside.

Meanwhile, bring several quarts of water to a boil in a large stockpot on the stovetop and cook the pasta until al dente. Transfer the pasta to a colander and rinse with cold water to stop the cooking. Drain thoroughly. Transfer the pasta to a large bowl.

Place the onions on a cutting board and slice. Cut the asparagus into 1-inch pieces. Add the onions and asparagus to the pasta and toss to combine. Drizzle with the dressing and toss again. Set aside for about an hour or so to allow the flavors to develop. Serve at room temperature. Pass grated Parmesan cheese, if desired.

Yield: 10 side-dish servings

Vermicelli with Grilled Tomato Sauce

INGREDIENTS

2 1/2 pounds (1.25 kilograms)
   pear tomatoes

2 medium onions

I large bulb garlic

2 tablespoons (28 milliliters)
   olive oil

6 teaspoons fresh oregano

I pound (455 grams) vermicelli

Grated Parmesan cheese
   (optional)

You might not think of grilling tomatoes, but this recipe will prove that they are delicious prepared this way. Serve with a garbanzo-bean salad and Bruschetta (page 67) for an unforgettable meal.

Preheat the grill to medium. Remove and discard the stem ends of the tomatoes, but leave them whole. Peel the onions and cut them in half. Break the garlic into individual cloves and peel them. Set the garlic aside.

Put the tomatoes directly on the grill. Rub the onions with 1 tablespoon of the olive oil and place them on the grill cut-side down. Grill the onions for about 30 minutes, turning occasionally, until tender. Turn the tomatoes frequently as they cook. (The skins will char and some of their juice will drip off.) Coat the garlic with the remaining tablespoon olive oil. Place the garlic in a grill basket and place on the grill for about 10 to 15 minutes, turning several times, until slightly charred and tender.

Remove the tomatoes, onions, and garlic from the grill and place in a food processor. Puree until slightly smooth. Add the oregano and puree to combine.

Meanwhile, bring several quarts of water to a boil in a large stockpot on the stovetop and cook the pasta until al dente. Drain the pasta and place it in a large serving bowl. Top with the sauce, toss gently, and serve immediately. Pass grated Parmesan cheese, if desired.

Yield: 6 main-dish servings

Fusilli Pasta in Caper Cream Sauce
with Grilled Eggplant and Red Bell Pepper Strips

INGREDIENTS

1 medium eggplant

3 teaspoons coarse salt

2 large red bell peppers

2 tablespoons (28 milliliters) olive oil

12 ounces (340 grams) fusilli pasta

1/3 cup (75 milliliters) dry white wine

3 tablespoons (45 grams) butter

3 tablespoons (25 grams) unbleached flour

1 3/4 cups (410 milliliters) whole milk

3 tablespoons (8 grams) minced fresh basil

3 tablespoons (25 grams) minced capers

Grated Parmesan cheese (optional)

The tartness of the capers in this recipe is the perfect compliment to the rich, creamy sauce.

Cut off the stem and bottom end of the eggplant and discard. Slice the eggplant crosswise into slices about 1/2-inch thick. To remove the eggplant's bitter juices, sprinkle both sides of the slices with the salt and place them on a rack for about 30 minutes. (The salt will cause the eggplant to "sweat" and release the bitter juices.) Briefly rinse the slices and blot them dry with paper towels.

Meanwhile, preheat the grill to medium-high. Place the bell peppers directly on the grill for 10 to 15 minutes, turning frequently. (The pepper skins will be charred black.) Transfer the peppers to a plastic or paper bag, close the bag, and set aside for about 15 minutes. When the peppers are cool enough to handle, peel off the skins and discard the seeds, stems, and white membranes. Coarsely chop the peppers and set aside in a warm spot.

Brush each side of the eggplant slices with the olive oil and place the slices on the grill. Grill for 5 to 8 minutes until lightly browned, turn, and continue to grill for another 5 to 8 minutes. (The eggplant should be tender-crisp, not mushy.) Remove the eggplant from the grill, cut into cubes, and set aside in a warm spot.

While the vegetables are grilling, fill a large stockpot with water for the pasta and place on the stovetop over high heat. Bring to a boil and add the pasta. Cook for 6 to 8 minutes, until al dente. Drain and place in a warm bowl.

While the pasta is cooking, heat the milk in a microwave or on the stovetop to scalding, but don't allow it to boil.

Melt the butter over medium heat in a heavy-bottomed skillet. Sift in the flour and cook for about a minute, whisking constantly. Add the hot milk, a little at a time, whisking constantly until it is incorporated. Continue to cook over medium-low heat for about 8 minutes. Add the wine, basil, and capers to the sauce. Stir in the eggplant and bell peppers. Heat through for a minute or two. Pour the sauce over the pasta. Gently toss to combine. Pass grated Parmesan cheese, if desired.

Yield: 4 main-dish servings

Marinated Grilled Eggplant
with Bowtie Pasta

INGREDIENTS

4 Japanese eggplants

2 tablespoons (28 milliliters)
  olive oil

2 cups (425 grams) cooked
  red beans

1 pound (455 grams)
  green beans

1/4 cup (60 milliliters)
  extra-virgin olive oil

2 tablespoons (28 milliliters)
  red wine vinegar

1 teaspoon crushed garlic

1/4 cup (10 grams) chopped
  fresh basil

1/4 cup (15 grams) chopped
  fresh flat-leaf parsley

6 teaspoons snipped fresh
  chives

1/4 teaspoon salt

1 pound (455 grams)
  bowtie pasta

2 ounces (55 grams)
  Parmesan cheese, shaved
  into thin strips

Eggplant soaks up flavor, so it is the perfect vegetable to carry the flavors of the fresh herbs in this outstanding pasta entrée. Choose the narrow, elongated eggplant variety—known as Japanese or Asian eggplant—for this dish. Use a kidney or another red bean variety to add a spark of color.

Preheat the grill to medium. Remove and discard the stem ends from the eggplants and slice lengthwise. Brush the cut sides of the eggplants with the olive oil and place on the grill skin sides down. Grill for 2 to 3 minutes, turn, and grill 2 to 3 minutes more. (The eggplant will develop grill marks and become slightly soft.) Remove the eggplants from the grill to a cutting board. Slice lengthwise and coarsely chop. Place the eggplant in a large bowl along with the red beans.

Trim the ends from the green beans and cut them into 1-inch pieces. Place the green beans on a steamer rack in a saucepan with a tight-fitting lid and cook on the stovetop over medium-high heat for 8 to 10 minutes, just until fork-tender. Drain the green beans and plunge them into ice water to stop the cooking and set their bright green color. Add the green beans to the bowl with the eggplant and red beans.

In a separate bowl, whisk together the extra-virgin olive oil, red wine vinegar, garlic, basil, parsley, chives, and salt. Pour the mixture over the eggplant and beans and marinate at room temperature for about an hour, tossing occasionally.

Bring several quarts of water to a boil in a large stockpot on the stovetop and cook the pasta until al dente. Transfer the pasta to a colander to drain. Place the pasta in a large shallow serving bowl and spoon the eggplant and beans over the top. Drizzle with all of the marinade left in the bowl. Gently toss to combine. Top with the Parmesan cheese and serve immediately.

Yield: 8 main-dish servings

Fettuccine with
Grilled Sweet-Potato Puree

INGREDIENTS

3 medium red-skinned sweet
potatoes

2 medium red bell peppers

2 cups (475 milliliters)
low-fat milk

2 tablespoons (28 grams)
unsalted butter

2 tablespoons (15 grams)
unbleached flour

1/4 teaspoon salt

Several grinds black pepper,
to taste

1/8 teaspoon freshly grated
nutmeg

1/4 teaspoon ground cinnamon

1 pound (455 grams) fettuccine

1/4 cup (60 milliliters) dry sherry

Grated Parmesan cheese
(optional)

This recipe was inspired by a dish that I enjoyed at a restaurant in New York City near Central Park. The thought of sweet potatoes and pasta had never occurred to me. This dish, with its red bell pepper garnish, is stunning on the plate, and it's simply delicious.

Preheat the grill to medium-high. Wash the sweet potatoes and pierce in several places with a fork. Place the sweet potatoes on the grill and grill for about 45 minutes, until they are soft, turning occasionally. Place the bell peppers on the grill. Cook for about 30 minutes, turning frequently to evenly char the skin. (The skins will blacken as they cook.) Remove the peppers, place them in a plastic or paper bag, and allow them to cool. When the peppers are cool enough to handle, peel off the blackened skins. Remove and discard the stems, seeds, and white membranes. Slice the peppers into 1/2-inch strips and set aside.

Remove the sweet potatoes from the grill and place them on a cutting board. Allow them to cool slightly, peel off the charred skins, and dice. Place them in a food processor with 1/2 cup of the milk and 1/4 cup (60 milliliters) water. Puree until smooth and set aside.

Meanwhile, put several quarts of water on to boil in a stockpot on the stovetop over high heat. On the stovetop, melt the butter in a large skillet over medium-low heat. Whisk in the flour, allow to cook a moment, and then gradually whisk in the remaining 1 1/2 cups milk. Add the salt, black pepper, nutmeg, and cinnamon. Cook the sauce for about 10 minutes, stirring frequently. Simultaneously, cook the fettuccine in the boiling water until al dente, about 8 to 10 minutes.

Add the sweet potato puree and sherry to the white sauce, whisk to combine, and heat through. Drain the fettuccine and place in a large warmed serving bowl. Toss with the sweet potato sauce and arrange the grilled bell pepper strips over the top. Serve immediately. Pass grated Parmesan cheese, if desired.

Yield: 6 main-dish servings

Pasta with Grilled Artichokes
and Fresh Shiitake Mushrooms

INGREDIENTS

3 medium artichokes

4 ounces (85 grams) fresh
   shiitake mushrooms

3 tablespoons (45 milliliters)
   olive oil

I teaspoon crushed garlic

I pound (455 grams) fusilli pasta

2 tablespoons (28 grams) butter

2 tablespoons (15 grams)
   unbleached flour

2 tablespoons (28 milliliters)
   dry sherry

I¹/2 cups (355 milliliters)
   low-fat milk

3 ounces (85 grams) coarsely
   grated Asiago cheese

3 teaspoons minced fresh
   tarragon

3 teaspoons minced flat-leaf
   parsley

¹/4 teaspoons salt

Several grinds black pepper,
   to taste

Grilled artichokes develop a subtle smoky flavor that pairs well with this pasta dish, complementing the strong flavor of the shiitake mushrooms.

Snap off the small, tough outer leaves at the base of the artichokes and trim off the pointy ends at the top. Trim and discard any sharp points from the mid-range leaves. Leave most of the stems, just trimming off the bottom ends. Put a steaming rack in a large saucepan and place the artichokes on the rack, leaves pointed down. Add several inches of water to the pan and cover tightly. Bring the water to a boil on the stovetop, reduce the heat to medium, and steam for about 25 minutes, until al dente. Remove the artichokes from the pan to a cutting board. Cool for several minutes. Using a sharp knife, cut the artichokes in half lengthwise. Spoon out and discard the chokes—the fuzzy fibers—leaving the leaves attached to the bottom.

Remove the stem ends from the mushrooms and place on a cutting board, gill sides up.

Place 2 tablespoons of the olive oil in a small bowl and whisk in the garlic. Distribute equal amounts of the oil mixture into the gills of each mushroom, reserving some to brush on the bottom side of each mushroom.

Meanwhile, preheat the grill to medium-high. Rub the cut sides of the artichokes with the remaining 1 tablespoon olive oil and place the artichokes cut sides down on the grill. Grill for about 2 minutes until grill marks appear, turn, and grill for 2 more minutes. Place the mushrooms on the grill, bottom sides down. Grill for 2 minutes, turn, and grill for 2 more minutes. Remove the artichokes and mushrooms from the grill and place on a platter. Set aside and keep warm.

Bring several quarts of water to a boil in a large stockpot on the stovetop for the pasta. Add the pasta and cook for 6 to 8 minutes, until al dente.

While the pasta is cooking, melt the butter in a skillet on the stovetop over medium-low heat, then stir in the flour and sherry. Cook for about 1 minute, stirring constantly, being careful not to scorch the flour. Add the milk, a bit at a time, whisking to incorporate as the sauce thickens. Stir in the Asiago cheese and allow it to melt. Add the tarragon, parsley, salt, and black pepper.

Drain the pasta and place it in a large shallow serving bowl. Pour the sauce over the top and toss to coat. Arrange the artichoke halves on top of the pasta, cut sides up. Cut the mushrooms into strips and distribute over the top of the pasta. Serve immediately.

Yield: 6 main-dish servings

Grilled Portobello Mushrooms
with Couscous and Gruyère Cheese

INGREDIENTS

1 cup (175 grams) uncooked couscous

2 jalapeño chiles, seeded and diced

1 tablespoon (14 grams) unsalted butter

$1/4$ teaspoon mild chili powder

$1/4$ teaspoon granulated garlic

4 medium portobello mushrooms

$1/4$ cup (60 milliliters) plus 1 teaspoon olive oil

2 tablespoons (28 milliliters) sweet chili sauce

$1/4$ cup (60 milliliters) dry white wine

1 cup (120 grams) loosely packed grated Gruyère cheese

6 teaspoons minced fresh cilantro

This recipe combines ingredients from many different cuisines, making it a real fusion dish. Most of the ingredients can be found readily at any supermarket, but you may need to go to an Asian market for the sweet chili sauce.

Place $1^1/2$ cups (355 milliliters) water in a saucepan on the stovetop and bring to a boil. Add the couscous, jalapeño chiles, butter, chili powder, and garlic. Stir to combine, cover, and then remove from the heat. Set aside for at least 5 minutes, undisturbed.

Meanwhile, preheat the grill to high with a smoker box in place. Remove the stem ends from the mushrooms and wipe the caps with a damp paper towel to remove any dirt. Place the mushrooms on a work surface, gill sides up. Evenly distribute the $1/4$ cup olive oil and sweet chili sauce over the gills of the mushrooms. Allow the mushrooms to absorb the olive oil mixture for about 15 minutes. Pour equal amounts of the wine into the gill side of each mushroom. Rub the bottom of the mushrooms with the reserved 1 teaspoon olive oil and transfer them to the grill, gill sides up. Grill for 3 to 4 minutes, turn, and continue to grill for an additional 3 to 4 minutes. Remove the mushrooms from the grill and place on a cutting board. Cut into thick slices.

To serve, place equal amounts of the couscous on 4 warm plates. Top with equal amounts of mushroom slices. Sprinkle with the Gruyère cheese and cilantro, then serve immediately.

Yield: 4 main-dish servings

Pasta with Grilled Fennel
and Asparagus

INGREDIENTS

- 1 bulb fennel, feathery tops removed
- 2 tablespoons (28 milliliters) olive oil
- 1 pound (455 grams) asparagus
- 12 ounces (340 grams) egg noodles
- 2 cups (475 milliliters) whole milk
- 3 tablespoons (45 grams) butter
- 1 shallot, finely minced
- 3 tablespoons (25 grams) unbleached flour
- 1/4 cup (13 grams) sun-dried tomatoes, reconstituted and minced
- 1/4 teaspoon salt
- Several grinds black pepper, to taste
- 1/4 teaspoon freshly grated nutmeg

The creamy sun-dried tomato sauce lightly coats the pasta and enhances the grilled vegetables in this dish. Nutmeg is the secret ingredient in this recipe; pass the nutmeg grinder at the table if you wish.

Preheat the grill to medium-high. Cut off and discard the top and bottom of the fennel and cut the bulb in half. Cut out and discard the inner core. Cut the halves into quarters and thinly slice. Place the fennel in a bag and add 1 tablespoon of the olive oil. Twist the bag to seal, allowing some air to remain in the bag. Toss gently to coat the fennel evenly. Place a grill grate on the grill and add the fennel from the bag. Grill for 8 to 10 minutes, turning the pieces occasionally. Remove the fennel from the grill and set aside in a warm spot.

Snap off and discard the tough ends from the asparagus and cut them into 1-inch pieces. Place the asparagus in the bag and add the remaining 1 tablespoon olive oil. Twist the bag to seal, allowing some air to remain in the bag. Toss gently to coat the asparagus evenly. Add the asparagus from the bag to the grill grate and cook, turning occasionally, for 8 to 10 minutes until tender crisp. Remove the asparagus from the grill and set aside in a warm spot.

Meanwhile, fill a large stockpot with water for the noodles and place on the stovetop over high heat. Bring to a boil and add the noodles. Cook for 6 to 8 minutes until al dente. Drain and place in a warm bowl.

While the pasta is cooking, heat the milk in a microwave or on the stovetop to scalding, but don't allow it to boil.

Melt the butter over medium heat in a heavy-bottomed skillet on the stovetop. Add the shallot and sauté for a minute or two. Sift in the flour and cook about a minute, whisking constantly. Add the hot milk a little at a time, whisking constantly until it is incorporated. Continue to cook over medium-low heat for about 10 minutes until thickened. Add the sun-dried tomatoes to the sauce. Stir in the salt, black pepper, and nutmeg. Pour over the drained noodles and toss to combine. Add the grilled fennel and asparagus, toss again, and serve immediately.

Yield: 6 main-dish servings

Lasagna with Grilled Corn,
Kalamata Olives, and Fresh Tomato Sauce

INGREDIENTS

2 pounds (1 kilogram) pear
   tomatoes

2 tablespoons (28 milliliters)
   olive oil

3 teaspoons crushed garlic

2 tablespoons (40 grams)
   honey

2 tablespoons (28 milliliters)
   red wine

6 teaspoons minced fresh
   oregano

2 ears corn, in husks

1 pound (455 grams) ricotta
   cheese

3/4 cup Grilled Kalamata Olives
   (page 61)

13 ounces (370 grams) fresh
   lasagna noodles

2 ounces (28 grams) fresh
   Parmesan cheese, thinly
   sliced

The corn, tomatoes, and cheese in this recipe meld together to create a light, summer-style lasagna. If you have a burner on your grill, you can prepare the entire dish outside. Many specialty markets sell fresh lasagna sheets. If you cannot locate fresh noodles and do not want to prepare them at home, use dried lasagna noodles and cook as instructed on the package before layering in this dish.

Cut the tomatoes in half crosswise and gently squeeze out the seed pockets. Coarsely chop the tomatoes and set aside.

Place the olive oil in a skillet over medium heat on the stovetop and add the garlic. Sauté for a minute, and then add the tomatoes. Increase the heat to medium-high and sauté for about 15 minutes, stirring occasionally. Add the honey, red wine, and oregano and continue to cook for about 10 more minutes.

Meanwhile, place the corn in a plastic bag and fill the bag with water to soak the husks for about 15 minutes. Preheat the grill to high. Remove the corn from the bag of water and place on the grill. Turn every few minutes to evenly blacken all sides of the husks. Grill for 18 to 22 minutes. (The kernels will steam in the husks.) Remove the corn from the grill. Allow the corn to cool, then peel off the husks and remove the silk. Cut the corn from the cob and set aside in a bowl. Mix in the ricotta cheese. Chop the Grilled Kalamata Olives and add them to the corn mixture, stirring to combine. Reduce the grill heat to medium-low.

Place $^1/_3$ of the tomato sauce evenly over the bottom of a 9-x-12-inch baking dish. Place a layer of noodles to cover, then half of the corn-ricotta mixture. Add another layer of noodles, $^1/_3$ more sauce, and the remaining corn-ricotta mixture. Top with the remaining noodles and tomato sauce. Cover with foil and place on the grill. Cook for 45 minutes, until the sauce is bubbling, then remove the foil and top with the Parmesan cheese. Continue to cook for about 10 minutes. Remove from the grill and cool for about 15 minutes before slicing into 6 equal portions.

Yield: 6 main-dish servings

Grilled Bok Choy
with Green Curry Rice

Curry paste is a wonderful, but spicy, ingredient. You will find prepared green, red, and yellow curry pastes in any Asian market. Use a small amount because the chili used as a major ingredient tends to be very hot! You can always add more if you like it spicy.

INGREDIENTS

1 pound (455 grams) baby bok choy

2 tablespoons (28 milliliters) pure sesame oil

1 cup (180 grams) uncooked basmati rice

14 ounces (400 milliliters) light coconut milk

2 teaspoons green curry paste

1 cup (235 milliliters) low-fat milk

Preheat the grill to medium-high. Rinse the bok choy and shake to remove some of the water. Cut any large heads in half lengthwise. Place the bok choy in a plastic bag and drizzle with the sesame oil. Twist the bag to seal, allowing some air to remain in the bag. Toss gently to coat the bok choy evenly. Remove the bok choy from the bag and place on the grill. Cook for 3 to 5 minutes, turning frequently, until the leaves are limp and slightly charred. Remove the bok choy from the grill, coarsely chop, and set aside.

Meanwhile, heat 2 cups (475 milliliters) water to a boil in a medium saucepan on the stovetop. Add the basmati rice, reduce the heat to low, and simmer for about 20 minutes. Remove the saucepan from the heat, fluff the rice with a fork, and set aside.

Place the coconut milk in a medium saucepan and whisk in the green curry paste. Heat over medium heat until just simmering and add the bok choy and milk. Cook for about 5 minutes.

Spoon equal amounts of rice into 4 individual serving bowls. Top each with equal amounts of the bok choy–curry mix. Serve immediately, with chutney and lemon slices.

Yield: 4 main-dish servings

Basmati Rice with
Grilled Summer Squashes

INGREDIENTS

6 small assorted summer
  squash

1 tablespoon (14 milliliters)
  olive oil

1 cup (180 grams) uncooked
  basmati rice

3 tablespoons (45 milliliters)
  extra-virgin olive oil

2 tablespoons (28 milliliters)
  red wine vinegar

1 teaspoon Dijon mustard

1/4 teaspoon salt

Several grinds black pepper,
  to taste

6 teaspoons chopped fresh
  oregano

1/2 pound (225 grams) cherry
  tomatoes, halved

4 green onions, thinly sliced

8 fresh squash blossoms
  (optional)

Use an assortment of small summer squashes to add color to this fragrant rice dish. If you grow squash, harvest eight squash blossoms to use as garnishes. You may also find fresh blossoms at your local farmers' market, or perhaps a generous gardening neighbor would be willing to share.

Preheat the grill to medium-high. Remove and discard the stem ends from the squashes and cut the squashes in half lengthwise. Place the squashes in a plastic bag and add the olive oil. Twist the bag to seal, allowing some of the air to remain in the bag. Toss gently to coat the squashes evenly. Remove the squashes from the bag and place them on the grill. Grill for 8 to 10 minutes until tender-crisp, turning twice. Remove the squashes from the grill, coarsely chop, and set aside.

Meanwhile, place 2 cups (475 milliliters) water in a saucepan on the stovetop and bring to a boil. Place the basmati rice in a fine mesh strainer and rinse, drain thoroughly, then stir it into the boiling water. Cover, reduce the heat to very low, and simmer for about 15 to 20 minutes until all of the water is absorbed. Turn off the heat and allow the saucepan to stand for at least 5 minutes before serving.

While the rice is cooking, whisk together the extra-virgin olive oil, red wine vinegar, mustard, salt, and black pepper until emulsified. Add the oregano and whisk again to combine. Set aside.

Place the rice in a shallow serving bowl. Add the grilled summer squashes, tomatoes, and green onions. Drizzle with the olive oil mixture and gently toss to combine. Garnish with the squash blossoms, if desired, and serve immediately.

Yield: 4 main-dish servings

Saffron Rice with
Grilled Fennel, Asparagus, and Leeks

INGREDIENTS

2 medium leeks

24 spears asparagus

1 bulb fennel

2 tablespoons (28 milliliters) olive oil

2 tablespoons (28 grams) unsalted butter

1½ cups (260 grams) uncooked long-grain white rice

¼ teaspoon saffron threads

1 tablespoon (14 milliliters) extra-virgin olive oil

1 tablespoon (14 milliliters) balsamic vinegar

Grated Parmesan cheese (optional)

Saffron adds a unique but delicate flavor to the rice in this dish, as well as a cheerful bright yellow color. The grilled vegetables are aromatic and have a tender-crisp texture.

Trim off and discard the green tops and root ends from the leeks. Cut the leeks in half lengthwise and thoroughly rinse each half to remove any sand. Set aside.

Snap off and discard the tough ends from the asparagus spears. Set aside.

Remove and discard the feathery top portion of the fennel. Slice the bulb in half lengthwise, then cut each half into 4 slices. Remove and discard the tough center cores. Set aside.

Preheat the grill to high with a smoker box in place. Put the fennel and leeks in a plastic bag and add 1 tablespoon of the olive oil. Twist the bag to seal, allowing some air to remain in the bag. Toss gently to coat the fennel and leeks evenly. Place a grill basket on the grill grate and add the fennel from the bag. Grill for 10 to 12 minutes until tender-crisp, turning several times. Meanwhile, add the leeks to the grill basket and grill for 8 to 10 minutes until tender-crisp, turning several times. Remove the fennel and leeks from the grill, place on a cutting board, tent with foil, and keep warm. Put the asparagus in the bag and drizzle with the remaining 1 tablespoon olive oil. Twist the bag to seal, allowing some air to remain in the bag. Toss gently to coat the asparagus evenly. Remove the asparagus from the bag, place on the grill, and cover the grill. Grill for 8 to 10 minutes, turning frequently, until the asparagus is al dente and slightly charred.

Meanwhile, place 3 cups (700 milliliters) water in a saucepan on the stovetop and bring to a boil. Add the butter and then stir in the rice. Crumble the saffron threads over the rice and stir to incorporate. Cover the saucepan, reduce the heat to very low, and cook for about 15 minutes, until the water is absorbed and the rice is tender. Remove from the heat.

Chop the grilled fennel, asparagus, and leeks, and drizzle with the extra-virgin olive oil and balsamic vinegar. Mound equal amounts of rice on 4 warm serving plates and top with the grilled vegetables. Serve immediately. Pass grated Parmesan cheese, if desired.

Yield: 4 main-dish servings

Grilled Zucchini
over Mint-Pesto Risotto

INGREDIENTS

3 medium zucchini

3 tablespoons (45 milliliters)
   olive oil

3 1/2 cups (830 ml) Vegetable
   Stock (page 25)

2 tablespoons (28 milliliters)
   dry white wine

2 shallots, minced

I cup (200 grams) uncooked
   Arborio rice

2/3 cup Mint Pesto (page 23)

Grated Romano cheese
   (optional)

The Mint Pesto (page 23) gives this dish a bright flavor and vibrant color. Use homemade Vegetable Stock (page 25) or a commercially prepared version.

Preheat the grill to medium-high. Remove and discard the stem ends from the zucchini and cut the zucchini lengthwise into 1/4-inch slices. Place the zucchini in a plastic bag and drizzle with 1 tablespoon of the olive oil. Twist the bag to seal, allowing some of the air to remain in the bag. Toss gently to coat the zucchini evenly. Place the zucchini on the grill and cook for about 10 minutes until tender-crisp, turning twice. Remove the zucchini from the grill, slice into matchsticks, and set aside.

Meanwhile, heat the Vegetable Stock in a saucepan on the stovetop until steaming and keep it handy near the stove.

Place the remaining 2 tablespoons olive oil and the wine in a heavy-bottomed saucepan on the stovetop over medium heat and add the shallots. Cook for about a minute, then add the rice. Stir to coat the rice. Add the stock, 1/2 cup at a time, stirring almost constantly and waiting until the liquid is absorbed before adding the next 1/2 cup. When the last 1/2 cup of stock has been absorbed and the rice is tender, remove from the heat and stir in the Mint Pesto.

Spoon the rice into bowls and top with equal amounts of the grilled zucchini strips. Serve immediately. Pass grated Romano cheese, if desired.

Yield: 4 main-dish servings

Pistachio-Encrusted Tofu
with Basmati Rice

INGREDIENTS

28 ounces (800 grams) extra-firm tofu

1 cup (180 grams) uncooked brown basmati rice

1/4 pound (115 grams) Cotswold cheese, sliced

1/2 cup (65 grams) minced pistachio nuts

2 tablespoons (28 milliliters) olive oil

2 tablespoons (28 grams) unsalted butter

2 tablespoons (15 grams) unbleached flour

1 cup Vegetable Stock (page 25)

1/2 cup Boysenberry Sauce (page 33)

My friend Lizz Blaise and I came up with the concept for this elegant presentation of tofu that tastes as good as it looks. If you cannot find Cotswold, an English cheese, use a sharp cheddar cheese instead. The drizzle of berry sauce on the plate and over the grilled tofu adds the final touch.

Cut the slabs of tofu through the middle to create 4 pieces. Place each piece on a paper towel and cover with another towel. Place a heavy skillet on top to press the excess water from the tofu. After 15 minutes, place the slabs between fresh towels and repeat the process.

Meanwhile, bring 2 cups (475 milliliter) water to a boil in a medium-sized saucepan on the stovetop. Put the basmati rice in a fine mesh strainer and rinse. Add the rice to the boiling water, return to a boil, reduce the heat to very low, cover, and simmer for 40 to 45 minutes, until all of the water is absorbed. Remove the saucepan from the heat and set aside until needed.

Preheat the grill to medium. Place the tofu on a work surface and place one-quarter of the Cotswold cheese on two of the slabs. Sprinkle with half of the nuts, then top with the remaining cheese. Cover with the remaining two slabs of tofu, as you would when making a sandwich, to create 2 cheese-filled tofu steaks. Brush the top and bottom of each steak with the olive oil. Press equal amounts of the remaining nuts into the outside of each steak, top and bottom. Place the tofu in a grill basket and clamp to encase the tofu steaks. Set aside.

Melt the butter in a skillet over low heat on the stovetop and whisk in the flour to form a thick paste. Increase the heat to medium and gradually add the Vegetable Stock, whisking to incorporate. Whisk in the Boysenberry Sauce and continue to cook until the sauce thickens, about 3 to 4 minutes. Cover and set aside.

Place the tofu steaks, in the grill basket, on the grill and grill for 4 to 6 minutes, turning several times. (The cheese will melt and the tofu will develop grill marks.) Drizzle 6 warm serving plates with some of the sauce. Cut the tofu steaks in thirds, creating 6 individual portions. Place one on each plate and drizzle with the remaining sauce. Pass the rice.

Yield: 6 main-dish servings

Risotto with Grilled Corn
and Red Peppers

INGREDIENTS

4 ears yellow corn, not husked

2 medium red bell peppers

3 1/2 cups (830 milliliters)
Vegetable Stock (page 25)

2 tablespoon (28 grams)
unsalted butter

2 cloves garlic, minced

1/4 teaspoon ground cumin

I teaspoon mild chili flakes

1/4 cup dry sherry

I cup (200 grams) uncooked
Arborio rice

1/4 cup (10 grams) chopped
fresh basil

Several grinds black pepper,
to taste

1/4 cup finely grated Parmesan
cheese

Fresh corn is a favorite summertime vegetable, so when it is in season, serve it in a variety of ways. Use homemade Vegetable Stock (page 25) or a commercially prepared version to flavor the risotto in this colorful dish.

Place the corn in a plastic bag and fill the bag with water to soak the husks for about 15 minutes. Meanwhile, heat the grill to high. Cut each bell pepper lengthwise from the stem to create 8 slices. Discard the stems, seeds, and white membranes. Place the peppers on the grill and grill for about 2 minutes per side, until they soften and char slightly. Remove the peppers from the grill. When the peppers are cool enough to handle, without peeling, coarsely chop and set aside.

Remove the corn from the bag and place directly on the grill. Turn every few minutes to evenly blacken all sides of the husks. Grill for 18 to 22 minutes. (The kernels will steam in the husks.) Remove the corn from the grill. When the corn is cool enough to handle, peel off the husks and silk. (Use a kitchen towel to hold the corn as you husk it if it is too hot to touch.) Return the corn to the grill to slightly char, turning and cooking for about 5 minutes. Working with one ear at a time, hold one end of the cob upright and place the other end on a cutting board. Take a sharp knife and cut the corn kernels from the cob, being careful not to cut through the cob itself. Place the kernels in a bowl and set aside.

Meanwhile, heat the Vegetable Stock in a saucepan on the stovetop until steaming and keep it handy near the stove.

Melt the butter in a heavy-bottomed saucepan on the stovetop over medium heat and add the garlic, cumin, and chili flakes. Cook for about a minute, then add the sherry and Arborio rice. Stir to coat the rice. Add the stock, 1/2 cup at a time, stirring almost constantly, and waiting until the liquid is absorbed before adding the next 1/2 cup. Add the corn and bell pepper with the last 1/2 cup of stock. When the last of the stock has been absorbed and the rice is tender, add the basil, black pepper, and Parmesan cheese. Stir to incorporate and serve immediately.

Yield: 4 main-dish servings

Portobello Mushrooms
in Mustard Marinade over Green Risotto

INGREDIENTS

1 cup (45 grams) lightly packed
  fresh basil

1 cup (30 grams) lightly packed
  fresh spinach

1/2 cup (120 milliliters) plus
  1/4 teaspoon olive oil

3 teaspoons crushed garlic

1/4 cup (65 grams) Dijon mustard

3 tablespoon (45 milliliters)
  extra-virgin olive oil

2 tablespoons (28 milliliters)
  freshly squeezed lemon juice

1/8 teaspoon salt

Several grinds black pepper,
  to taste

4 small portobello mushrooms

1 tablespoon (14 grams) butter

2 tablespoon (28 milliliters)
  cooking sherry

1 cup (200 grams) uncooked
  Arborio rice

3 1/2 cups (830 milliliters)
  Vegetable Stock (page 25)

Fresh basil and spinach give the risotto in this recipe its green color. The mustard-infused portobello mushrooms finish the dish.

Place the basil, spinach, 1/2 cup olive oil, and 1 teaspoon of the garlic in a food processor and puree. Set aside.

Combine the mustard, extra-virgin olive oil, lemon juice, salt, and black pepper in a bowl and whisk together.

Cut off the stem ends of the mushrooms and reserve for another use. With the gill sides up, distribute equal amounts of the mustard sauce in each mushroom. Marinate for about 10 minutes.

Meanwhile, melt the butter in a heavy-bottomed saucepan on the stovetop and add the sherry. Add the Arborio rice and stir to coat. Add the Vegetable Stock, 1/2 cup at a time, stirring almost constantly and waiting until the liquid is absorbed before adding the next 1/2 cup. Add the basil puree with the last 1/2 cup of stock.

While the rice is cooking, preheat the grill to medium-high. Rub the 1/4 teaspoon olive oil on the cap sides of the mushrooms and place them on the grill, cap sides down (gill sides up). Grill for 8 to 10 minutes, until fork-tender. Remove the mushrooms from the grill, slice, and briefly set aside in a warm spot.

Spoon the risotto into 4 warm shallow bowls. Arrange the mushroom slices on top and serve immediately.

Yield: 4 main-dish servings

Grilled Polenta
with Tomato Coulis

INGREDIENTS

$^1/_2$ teaspoon dried thyme

1 teaspoon salt

1 cup (125 grams) uncooked
  polenta

$^1/_3$ cup (35 grams) finely grated
  Parmesan cheese

2 tablespoons (28 grams)
  unsalted butter

1 tablespoon (14 milliliters)
  olive oil

1 cup (235 milliliters) Tomato
  Coulis (page 24)

Grated Parmesan cheese
  (optional)

You can serve this grilled polenta in many ways. When tomatoes are in season, the fresh Tomato Coulis (page 24) is the perfect topping. During the winter, you may want to serve it with a mushroom sauce. The polenta does require some time to set up before grilling, so prepare it in advance. Serve this with a grilled or steamed seasonal vegetable and a light red wine.

Bring 2 cups (475 milliliters) water to a boil in a heavy-bottomed saucepan on the stovetop over medium-high heat. Crush the thyme between the palms of your hands, then add it to the water along with the salt. Gradually pour in the polenta in a slow, steady stream, whisking constantly. Reduce the heat to medium-low and gently simmer for about 20 minutes, stirring almost constantly with a wooden spoon. (The polenta will thicken as it cooks.) Add the Parmesan cheese and butter during the last few minutes of cooking time. When the polenta is thick enough to pull away from the sides of the pan, pour the polenta into a small loaf pan and set aside to firm up for about 30 minutes. (You may set it aside for several hours, depending on your time frame.)

Preheat the grill to medium-high. Slice the polenta into 4 thick slices, or 8 thinner ones, depending on the size of the pan that you used as the mold. Brush the polenta slices with the olive oil and place on the grill. Grill for 5 to 6 minutes, turn, and continue to grill for 4 to 5 minutes. (The slices will develop grill marks.)

Meanwhile, heat the Tomato Coulis in a small saucepan.

Place the grilled polenta slices on individual warmed serving plates and top with the Tomato Coulis. Pass additional grated Parmesan cheese, if desired.

Yield: 4 main-dish servings

Polenta with Broccoli Rabe
and Portobello Mushrooms

INGREDIENTS

I large red bell pepper

I cup (125 grams) uncooked polenta

$^1/_2$ cup (60 grams) grated Monterey Jack cheese

$^1/_4$ cup (25 grams) finely grated Parmesan cheese

2 large portobello mushrooms

$^1/_2$ cup (120 milliliters) olive oil

$^1/_2$ cup Soy and Balsamic Fusion Marinade (page 26)

4 cloves garlic, minced

I$^1/_2$ teaspoons lemon juice

I$^1/_2$ pounds (700 grams) broccoli rabe

This delicious meal comes together in several stages. You can make the sauce in advance and set it aside. Prepare the polenta and keep it warm, covered, or enlist help to prepare it while you grill the mushrooms and broccoli rabe. The presentation is beautiful.

Preheat the grill to medium-high. Place the bell pepper directly on the grill and cook for 10 to 15 minutes, turning frequently. Grill until the skin is charred black. Transfer the pepper to a plastic or paper bag, close the bag, and set aside for about 15 minutes. When the pepper is cool enough to handle, remove and discard the stem end, seeds, and white membrane. Dice the pepper and set aside.

Heat 4 cups (1 liter) water to a boil in a medium sauce pan on the stovetop. Gradually pour in the polenta in a slow, steady stream, whisking constantly. Reduce the heat to medium-low and simmer for about 20 minutes, stirring almost constantly with a wooden spoon. When the polenta is thick enough to begin to pull away from the sides of the pan, add the Monterey Jack cheese, Parmesan cheese, and bell pepper. Stir to combine. Cover and keep warm until serving. Stir in a tablespoon or two of hot water just before serving if the polenta appears to be too thick.

Meanwhile, cut off the stem ends of the mushrooms and set aside for another use. Lightly rub a small amount of olive oil on the cap side of the mushrooms. With the gill sides up, distribute 2 tablespoons of the Soy and Balsamic Fusion Marinade into each mushroom. Place the mushrooms cap sides down (gill sides up) on the grill and grill 8 to 10 minutes, until fork-tender. Remove from the grill and briefly set aside. Cut into slices before serving.

While the mushrooms are cooking, whisk together the olive oil, garlic, and lemon juice. Place the broccoli rabe on a platter and drizzle with the oil mixture. Place the broccoli rabe on the grill and grill 3 to 5 minutes, until wilted. Turn frequently. Remove the broccoli rabe from the grill, then trim off and discard the stem ends. Fan the broccoli rabe onto 4 warm plates. Top with equal amounts of polenta and mushroom slices. Serve immediately.

Yield: 4 main-dish servings

Grilled Onions and Zucchini
with Gorgonzola Polenta

INGREDIENTS

2 small yellow onions

2 tablespoons (28 milliliters)
  olive oil

3 medium zucchini

1 tablespoon (14 milliliters)
  balsamic vinegar

2 teaspoons crushed garlic

$^1/_4$ teaspoon salt

1 cup (125 grams) uncooked
  polenta

2 tablespoons (28 grams)
  unsalted butter

3 tablespoons (10 grams) fresh
  sage leaves, minced

2 ounces (55 grams) crumbled
  Gorgonzola cheese

Fresh sage leaves (optional)

This soft, creamy polenta is the perfect base for the balsamic-infused onions and zucchini. This dish has several steps, but it comes together easily—and it's delicious!

Preheat the grill to medium-high. Trim off the ends of the onions and peel them, then cut in half across the middle. Rub 1 table-spoon of the olive oil over the cut ends. Place the onions, cut sides down, directly on the grill. Grill for 25 to 30 minutes, turning every 8 to 10 minutes. (The onions are done when they are soft and slightly charred.)

Meanwhile, remove and discard the stem ends from the zucchini and cut lengthwise into $^1/_4$-inch slices. Place the zucchini in a plastic bag and add the remaining 1 tablespoon olive oil, the balsamic vinegar, 1 teaspoon garlic, and the salt. Twist the bag to seal, allow-ing some of the air to remain in the bag. Toss gently to coat the zucchini evenly. Remove the zucchini from the bag, place on the grill, and cook for about 10 minutes, until tender-crisp, turning twice.

While the vegetables are cooking, bring 4 cups (1 liter) water to a boil in a saucepan on the stovetop over medium-high heat for the polenta. Add the remaining 1 teaspoon garlic, then whisk in the polenta, adding it in a slow, steady stream. Reduce the heat to low and gently simmer for about 20 minutes, stirring almost constantly with a wooden spoon. (As it cooks, the polenta will thicken.)

Melt the butter in a small pan over medium-low and add the sage. Cook for about 3 to 4 minutes, remove from the heat, and set aside. When the polenta is done, strain the sage butter into it, discarding the sage. Stir in the Gorgonzola cheese and mix to combine.

Spoon equal amounts of polenta onto 4 warm serving plates. Place half of an onion on each plate and arrange equal amounts of zucchini over each portion of polenta. Garnish with additional fresh sage, if you wish. Serve immediately.

Yield: 4 main-dish servings

Grilled Corn and
Cheddar Cheese Polenta

This recipe has several steps, but the results are worth the effort. Serve with Salsa Fresca (page 45) or your favorite commercially prepared salsa.

INGREDIENTS

2 ears corn, not husked

2 tablespoons (28 grams) butter

2 jalapeño chiles, seeded and minced

1 1/2 cups (190 grams) uncooked polenta

8 ounces (225 grams) grated cheddar cheese

1 teaspoon granulated garlic

1/2 teaspoon salt

1 teaspoon mild chili powder

Salsa Fresca (page 45) or prepared salsa

Place the corn in a plastic bag and fill the bag with water to soak the husks for about 15 minutes. Meanwhile, preheat the grill to high. Remove the corn from the bag of water and place on the grill. Turn every few minutes to evenly blacken all sides of the husks. Grill for 18 to 22 minutes. (The kernels will steam in the husks.) Remove the corn from the grill. Allow the corn to cool, then peel off the husks and remove the silk. Cut the kernels from the cob and set aside in a bowl.

Meanwhile, melt the butter over low heat in a large saucepan on the stovetop and add the jalapeño chiles. Sauté for a couple of minutes, then add 6 cups (1.5 liters) hot water. Increase the heat to high and bring to a boil. Gradually pour in the polenta in a slow, steady stream, whisking constantly. Reduce the heat to medium-low and gently simmer for about 20 minutes, stirring almost constantly with a wooden spoon. (The polenta will thicken as it cooks.) Add the cheddar cheese and corn during the last few minutes of cooking time, along with the garlic, salt, and chili powder. When the polenta is thick enough to pull away from the sides of the pan, pour into 8 individual 4-inch ramekins and allow to firm up for about 30 minutes. (You may set the ramekins aside for several hours, depending on your time frame.)

Run a thin knife blade around the rim of each ramekin and turn the polenta out onto a cutting board. Place the polenta directly on the grill and grill for about 3 minutes on each side, turning with a wide spatula. Remove the polenta from the grill and serve immediately, passing your favorite salsa.

Yield: 8 main-dish servings

Grilled Eggplant Parmesan
with Soft Polenta

The eggplant in this dish is grilled, not fried, providing the perfect base for the tomato and Parmesan cheese to be served upon.

INGREDIENTS

I medium eggplant

3 teaspoons coarse salt

1¼ pounds (570 grams) pear
   tomatoes

3 tablespoons (45 milliliters)
   olive oil

2 cloves garlic, minced

¼ teaspoon salt

2 tablespoons (28 milliliters)
   red wine

3 teaspoons minced fresh oregano

2 ounces (55 grams) Parmesan
   cheese, shaved into thin strips

I cup (125 grams) uncooked
   polenta

½ cup (100 grams) finely grated
   Parmesan cheese

I tablespoon (14 grams) unsalted
   butter

Fresh oregano sprigs (optional)

Cut off the stem and bottom ends of the eggplant and slice crosswise into slices about ½-inch thick. To rid the eggplant of its bitter juices, sprinkle both sides of the slices with the coarse salt and place them on a rack for about 30 minutes. (The salt will cause the eggplant to "sweat" and release the bitter juices.) Briefly rinse the eggplant and blot dry with paper towels.

Meanwhile, cut the tomatoes in half crosswise and gently squeeze out the seed pockets. Chop the tomatoes coarsely and set side.

Heat 1 tablespoon of the olive oil in a sauté pan over medium heat on the stovetop and add the garlic. Stir and sauté briefly, then add the tomatoes and salt. Cook, uncovered, over medium-high heat for about 10 minutes, until the tomatoes are soft and have released their liquid. Stir in the red wine and oregano and continue to cook for about 5 minutes, until a chunky sauce develops. Set aside.

Preheat the grill to high. Brush each side of the eggplant slices with the remaining 2 tablespoons olive oil and place on the grill. Grill the eggplant for 5 to 8 minutes until browned, turn, and continue to grill for another 5 to 8 minutes. Remove the eggplant from the grill to a large platter. Top with equal amounts of the tomato sauce and distribute the shaved Parmesan cheese over the sauce. Set the eggplant aside in a warm spot.

Heat 4 cups (1 liter) water to a boil in a medium saucepan on the stovetop. Gradually pour in the polenta in a slow, steady stream, whisking constantly. Reduce the heat to medium-low and simmer for about 20 minutes, stirring almost constantly with a wooden spoon. When the polenta is thick enough to begin to pull away from the sides of the pan, add the grated Parmesan cheese and butter. Stir to combine. Cover and keep warm until needed. Stir in a tablespoon or two of hot water just before serving if the polenta appears to be too thick.

Carefully place the eggplant slices back on the grill and heat for about 2 minutes to warm them. To serve, place equal amounts of polenta on 6 warm plates. Flatten slightly, then top with eggplant slices. Garnish with oregano sprigs, if desired.

Yield: 6 main-dish servings

CHAPTER 8

Skewered Entrées

Skewered entrées are easy to prepare and elegant to serve. Wooden skewers are best for tofu dishes, because the succulent ingredients may fall apart when skewered with sharp metal skewers. Soak wooden skewers in water for at least 10 minutes before threading with the recipe ingredients to prevent the skewers from scorching on the grill. If they begin to burn while the ingredients are cooking, place a strip of foil on the grill under the ends of the skewers to prevent the heat from singing them. If you use metal skewers, the cooking time will be slightly less, as the metal will transmit heat to the food from within.

Food cooks quickly on skewers, but some of the recipes require time for the ingredients to marinate. Prepare the marinades in advance and allow the ingredients to soak up the delicious flavors. Tofu Sates (page 167) and Curry-Marinated Tofu Skewers with Jalapeño and Lime (page 161) are sure to become favorites. Reserve the marinade to pour over the skewers as they grill or pour over the entrée when served.

Dipping sauces are the perfect accompaniment to serve with skewered entrées because the cubes of food are just the right size for dipping. I've made suggestions in some of the recipes, but read through "Salsas, Chutneys, and Dipping Sauces," beginning on page 34, for additional ideas. Serve the Dilled Yogurt and Sour Cream Sauce (page 51) with Tofu in Garlic-Soy Marinade (page 168), and try the Spicy Tahini Sauce (page 50) with Tempeh, Mushroom, and Cherry Tomato Skewers (page 165).

Have the rest of the meal prepared and just about ready to serve when you put the skewers on the grill. Spray or brush some oil on the grill rack, then place the skewers crosswise on the grill. Most skewered entrées cook in just 15 to 20 minutes, but they need to be turned several times while they are cooking. Some recipes call for two skewers to be threaded side by side so the ingredients will not twist around on the skewers. Serve the skewers on a large warm platter or on individual serving plates. Allow diners to remove the grilled ingredients from the skewers at the table.

Tempeh, Pineapple, and Jalapeño Skewers

INGREDIENTS

1/2 cup (120 milliliters) unsweetened coconut milk

2 tablespoons (28 milliliters) unseasoned rice vinegar

1 tablespoon (14 milliliters) toasted sesame oil

1 tablespoon (14 milliliters) soy sauce

8 ounces (225 grams) soy tempeh, cut into 24 cubes

6 jalapeño chiles, cubed

1 cup (155 grams) cubed pineapple

8 ounces (225 grams) soba noodles

Serve these skewers with Peanut Sauce (page 46) or Mango and Papaya Salsa with Jalapeños (page 37) to bring all of the flavors together. Soba noodles are made with buckwheat flour, and they're delicious with this dish.

Soak 8 wooden skewers in water. Place the coconut milk, rice vinegar, sesame oil, and soy sauce in a medium bowl and whisk together. Pour into a loaf pan and add the tempeh. Gently toss to combine. Set aside to marinate for about 30 minutes.

Preheat the grill to medium-high. Start with a cube of jalapeño chile and alternately thread the tempeh and pineapple on each skewer. End with a cube of jalapeño pepper. Repeat with the remaining ingredients to fill all 8 skewers. Place the skewers on the grill and grill for 12 minutes, turning several times. Spoon some of the reserved marinade over the skewers while they grill. Reserve the remaining marinade to spoon over the soba noodles when they are served.

Meanwhile, in a large stockpot, heat several quarts of water to a boil over high heat on the stovetop. Add the soba noodles and stir gently, bring back to a boil, and cook for about 5 minutes, until the soba noodles are tender but not mushy. Drain well and distribute between 4 warm serving plates.

Top each with two tempeh skewers and serve immediately. Drizzle with any remaining marinade.

Yield: 4 main-dish servings

Zucchini, Onion, and Red Bell Pepper Skewers

INGREDIENTS

1 pound (455 grams) pearl onions

2 large red bell peppers

1 pound (455 grams) zucchini, cut into 1-inch rounds

1/4 cup (60 milliliters) olive oil

1 tablespoon (14 milliliters) balsamic vinegar

2 teaspoons crushed garlic

1/4 teaspoon salt

Dilled Yogurt and Sour Cream Sauce (page 51)

Crusty fresh bread or Bruschetta (page 67)

Various cheeses

Summer gardens provide us with so much fresh produce—such a treat for us to grill! When the garden is overflowing, invite a few friends over and prepare this simple dish. Use yellow and green zucchini and red and yellow peppers for a particularly pleasing presentation. Serve with Dilled Yogurt and Sour Cream Sauce (page 51). Pass crusty fresh bread or Bruschetta (page 67) and a selection of cheeses.

Soak 12 wooden skewers in water. Put several quarts of water in a large saucepan and heat to a boil on the stovetop. Place the onions in a blanching basket, place it in the boiling water, bring back to a boil and cook for about a minute. Plunge the onions into cold water and slip off the skins. Leave the onions whole and set aside.

Preheat the grill to medium-high with a smoker box in place. Stem and seed the bell peppers and cut into 1-inch cubes. Place the onions, bell peppers, and zucchini in a plastic bag. Drizzle with the olive oil and balsamic vinegar and add the garlic. Twist the bag to seal, allowing some of the air to remain in the bag. Toss gently to coat the vegetables evenly.

Start with a cube of bell pepper and alternately thread the onions and zucchini on each skewer. Repeat with the remaining skewers to fill all 12 skewers. Place on the grill and grill for 12 to 15 minutes, turning several times.

Place the skewers on a large warm platter. Put individual plates on the table for your guests. Serve the Dilled Yogurt and Sour Cream Sauce along with the bread or Bruschetta and cheeses of your choice.

Yield: 6 main-dish servings

Red Potato and
Mushroom Skewers

This is a good recipe to prepare at any time of year. The Basil Pesto (page 23) pasta forms a flavorful base for the grilled vegetables, and the presentation is beautiful.

INGREDIENTS

- 1¼ pounds (570 grams) small red potatoes
- ¼ cup (60 milliliters) olive oil
- ¾ pound (340 grams) small button mushrooms
- 1 teaspoon soy sauce
- 1 teaspoon crushed garlic
- ½ cup Basil Pesto (page 23)
- ¼ cup (60 grams) sour cream
- ½ pound (225 grams) capellini pasta
- Grated Parmesan cheese (optional)

Soak 6 wooden skewers in water. Preheat the grill to medium-high. Scrub the potatoes but do not peel them. Place the potatoes in the microwave oven and cook them for about 5 minutes, until slightly soft but not completely cooked. (They will finish cooking on the grill.) When the potatoes are cool enough to handle, cut them into uniform chunks. Set the potatoes aside in a medium bowl and drizzle with 2 tablespoons of the olive oil.

Meanwhile, brush the dirt from the mushrooms and trim the stem ends to be flush with the bottom of each mushroom. Reserve the stems for another use.

In a medium bowl, whisk together the remaining 2 tablespoons olive oil and the soy sauce and garlic. Place the mushrooms in the bowl and toss to combine. Set aside.

Place the Basil Pesto in a small bowl and whisk in the sour cream. Set aside.

Bring several quarts of water to a boil in a large stockpot on the stovetop for the pasta. Skewer the potatoes and mushrooms, alternating them on the skewers, and set aside. Add the pasta to the pot of boiling water and cook for 6 to 8 minutes, until al dente. While the pasta is cooking, place the skewers on the grill and grill for 6 to 8 minutes, turning several times.

Whisk ¼ cup (60 milliliters) of the pasta cooking water into the pesto mixture. Drain the pasta in a colander and place it in a shallow bowl. Add the pesto mixture and toss to combine. Place equal amounts of pasta on 6 warm serving plates. Top with skewers of potatoes and mushrooms and serve immediately. Pass grated Parmesan cheese, if desired.

Yield: 6 main-dish servings

Curry-Marinated Tofu Skewers
with Jalapeño and Lime

INGREDIENTS

1/2 cup (120 milliliters)
  unsweetened coconut milk

2 tablespoons (28 milliliters)
  freshly squeezed lime juice

1 tablespoon (14 milliliters)
  toasted sesame oil

2 teaspoons curry powder

1/4 teaspoon salt

28 ounces (800 grams)
  extra-firm tofu

4 limes

4 jalapeño chiles, sliced

1 cup (180 grams) uncooked
  basmati rice

Dilled Yogurt and Sour Cream
  Sauce (page 51)
  (optional)

Tofu will accept almost any flavor, and here curry is the star. Serve this Middle Eastern-inspired dish with Dilled Yogurt and Sour Cream Sauce (page 51).

Soak 8 wooden skewers in water. In a small bowl, whisk together the coconut milk, lime juice, sesame oil, curry powder, and salt. Set aside.

Cut the slabs of tofu through the middles to create 4 pieces. Place each piece on a paper towel, cover with another towel, and place a heavy skillet on top to remove excess moisture. After 15 minutes, place the slabs between fresh towels and repeat the process. Cut each slab into 6 pieces to form cubes.

Place about half of the curry marinade in a shallow baking dish and add the tofu in a single layer. Pour the remainder of the marinade over the top. Marinate for about an hour, gently turning the pieces after about 30 minutes.

Preheat the grill to medium-high. Cut each lime into 8 wedges. Start with a lime wedge and alternately thread the tofu, jalapeño chiles, and lime wedges on each skewer, ending with a lime wedge, to create 8 threaded skewers. Reserve any residual marinade. Place the skewers on the grill and grill for about 20 minutes, turning several times.

Meanwhile, bring 2 cups (475 milliliters) water to a boil in a medium-sized saucepan on the stovetop. Put the basmati in a fine mesh strainer and rinse. Add the rice to the boiling water, return to a boil, reduce the heat to very low, cover, and simmer for 15 to 20 minutes, until all of the water is absorbed.

Mound equal amounts of rice on 4 warm serving plates and top each serving with 2 skewers. Drizzle with any remaining curry marinade. Serve with the Dilled Yogurt and Sour Cream Sauce, if desired.

Yield: 4 main-dish servings

Skewered Tofu and Tomatoes

INGREDIENTS

28 ounces (800 grams) extra-firm
tofu

Honey-Ginger Marinade (page 27)

1/2 pound (225 grams) cherry
tomatoes

I cup (140 grams) uncooked bulgur

This is a fast, simple dish that is perfect with a fresh green salad. I always use extra-firm tofu, since it can be cut into cubes and skewered without falling apart. Choose a mixture of different colors of cherry tomatoes (red, yellow, orange) for a stunning presentation.

Soak 16 wooden skewers in water. Cut the slabs of tofu through the middle to create 4 pieces. Place each piece on a paper towel, cover with another towel, and place a heavy skillet on top to remove excess moisture. After 15 minutes, place the slabs between fresh towels to repeat the process. Cut each slab into 6 pieces to form cubes.

Place about half of the Honey-Ginger Marinade in a shallow baking dish and add the tofu in a single layer. Pour the remainder of the marinade over the top. Marinate for about an hour, gently turning the pieces after about 30 minutes.

Preheat the grill to high. Using 2 skewers per serving, place them about 1/2-inch apart, threading each piece onto both skewers at once. Start with a tomato and alternately thread the tofu and tomatoes on each skewer to create 8 double-threaded skewers. Reserve any residual marinade. Place the skewers on the grill and grill for about 20 minutes, turning several times.

Meanwhile, bring 2 cups (475 milliliters) water to a boil in a medium-sized saucepan on the stovetop. Add the bulgur, return to a boil, reduce the heat to very low, cover, and simmer for 15 minutes. Turn off the heat without disturbing the lid and set aside for 5 minutes.

Mound equal amounts of bulgur on 4 warm serving plates and top each serving with 2 skewers. Drizzle with the reserved marinade.

Yield: 4 main-dish servings

Spicy Peanut Tofu Skewers
with a Trio of Bell Peppers

INGREDIENTS

1/2 cup (130 grams) smooth
  peanut butter

6 tablespoons (90 milliliters)
  dry sake

1/4 cup (60 milliliters) freshly
  squeezed lemon juice

2 tablespoons (28 milliliters)
  peanut oil

3 teaspoons chili flakes

28 ounces (800 grams)
  extra-firm tofu

I pound (455 grams) bell
  peppers

I cup (180 grams) uncooked
  jasmine rice

Use green, red, and yellow bell peppers for this tasty and colorful entrée. The marinade is spicy, so if you prefer a milder dish, use half the amount of chili flakes. You can serve this with a dipping sauce, if desired.

Soak 8 bamboo skewers in water. In a small bowl, whisk together the peanut butter, sake, lemon juice, peanut oil, and chili flakes. Set aside.

Cut the slabs of tofu through the middle to create 4 pieces. Place each piece on a paper towel, cover with another towel, and place a heavy skillet on top to remove excess moisture. After 15 minutes, place the slabs between fresh towels to repeat the process. Cut each slab into 6 pieces to form cubes.

Place about half of the peanut marinade in a shallow baking dish and add the tofu in a single layer. Pour the remainder of the marinade over the top. Marinate for about an hour, gently turning the pieces after about 30 minutes.

Remove and discard the stem ends of the bell peppers and cut them in half. Cut out and discard the membrane and seeds. Slice the halves in half and then into about 1-inch cubes.

Preheat the grill to medium-high. Skewer the bell peppers and tofu, starting with a bell-pepper cube, and alternately thread the tofu and bell-pepper cubes, ending with a bell-pepper cube, to create 8 threaded skewers. Reserve any residual marinade. Place the skewers on the grill and grill for about 20 minutes, turning several times.

Meanwhile, bring 2 cups (475 milliliters) water to a boil in a medium-sized saucepan on the stovetop. Put the jasmine rice in a fine mesh strainer and rinse. Add the rice to the boiling water, return to a boil, reduce the heat to very low, cover, and simmer for 15 to 20 minutes until all of the water is absorbed. Mound equal amounts of rice on 4 warm serving plates and top each serving with 2 skewers. Drizzle with any reserved marinade.

Yield: 4 main-dish servings

Tempeh, Mushroom, and Cherry Tomato Skewers

INGREDIENTS

^{1}/4 cup (60 milliliters) dry sake

3 tablespoons (45 milliliters) soy sauce

2 tablespoons (28 milliliters) sesame oil

3 teaspoons grated fresh ginger

2 teaspoons dry wasabi

2 teaspoons rice vinegar

16 ounces (455 grams) soy tempeh

1^1/2 cups (270 grams) uncooked brown basmati rice

^{1}/2 pound (225 grams) cremini mushrooms

1 pound (455 grams) cherry tomatoes

Spicy Tahini Sauce (page 50)

Creamy Ponzu Sauce (page 51)

The flavors in this easy dish blend to create a delicious and satisfying entrée. The ginger in the marinade adds a delightful fragrance to the kitchen as the tempeh marinates. Choose cherry tomatoes in variety of different colors for a particularly pleasing presentation. Serve with Spicy Tahini Sauce (page 50) or Creamy Ponzu Sauce (page 51).

Soak 12 wooden skewers in water. Place the sake, soy sauce, sesame oil, and ginger in a small bowl and whisk together.

In a separate small bowl, whisk together the wasabi and rice vinegar to form a paste. Add to the sake mixture, whisk to combine the two, and set aside.

Cut the tempeh into 40 small squares. Put the squares in a shallow pan and pour the sake mixture over them. Marinate for about 30 minutes, tossing occasionally.

Meanwhile, place 3 cups (700 milliliters) water in a saucepan over high heat on the stovetop. Bring to a boil. Rinse the rice, stir it into the water, return to a boil, cover, and reduce the heat to very low. Simmer for about 45 minutes, then turn off the heat and allow to sit undisturbed for at least 5 minutes.

Preheat the grill to medium. Remove the stems from the mushrooms and reserve for another use. Thickly slice the mushrooms. Start with a cherry tomato and alternately thread the tempeh, mushrooms, and cherry tomatoes on the skewers, ending with a cherry tomato. Repeat with the remaining ingredients to fill all 12 skewers. Reserve the marinade. Place the skewers on the grill and grill for 10 minutes, turning several times. Pour the reserved marinade over the skewers as they grill.

Place equal amounts of rice on 6 warm serving plates. Top each serving with 2 skewers. Serve the Spicy Tahini Sauce or Creamy Ponzu Sauce dipping sauces as desired.

Yield: 6 main-dish servings

Tofu Sates

INGREDIENTS

28 ounces (800 grams)
  extra-firm tofu

3 stalks lemon grass

2 cloves garlic, minced

I Thai chile or jalapeño chile,
  seeded and minced

I teaspoon ground coriander

1/2 teaspoon ground turmeric

2 tablespoons (28 milliliters)
  freshly squeezed lime juice

3/4 cup (175 milliliters)
  unsweetened coconut milk

3 tablespoons (45 milliliters)
  soy sauce

2 tablespoons (40 grams)
  honey

I cup (185 grams) uncooked
  long-grain brown rice

Peanut Sauce (page 46) or
  Creamy Ponzu Sauce
  (page 51) (optional)

Sates are small kebabs on a stick. I make this tofu version by marinating the tofu in a rich sauce that is a combination of coconut milk, spices, and minced Thai chile or jalapeño chiles. Prepare your own sauce as shown below or purchase a commercially prepared version from the supermarket or Asian market. I like to serve this as an entrée, but it is also a delightful appetizer. Serve it with Peanut Sauce (page 46) or Creamy Ponzu Sauce (page 51) if you wish.

Soak 8 wooden skewers in water. Cut the slabs of tofu through the middle to create 4 pieces. Place each piece on paper towel, cover with another towel, and place a heavy skillet on top to remove excess moisture. After 15 minutes, place the slabs between fresh towels to repeat the process. Cut each slab into 6 pieces to form cubes.

Meanwhile, trim off and discard the root ends and top green ends from the lemon grass stalks. Discard the tough outer layers and mince the tender inner cores.

Place the lemon grass, garlic, Thai chile or jalapeño chile, coriander, and turmeric in a mortar and use the pestle to pound into a fragrant paste. Add the lime juice and pound to combine. Transfer to a ceramic or glass bowl and stir in the coconut milk, soy sauce, and honey.

Place half of the sauce in a shallow baking dish and add the tofu. Pour the remaining sauce over the top. Marinate for about an hour, gently turning the cubes after about 30 minutes.

Meanwhile, place 2 1/4 cups (525 milliliters) water in a saucepan on the stovetop and bring to a boil. Add the rice, cover the saucepan, and reduce the heat to very low. Cook for 40 to 45 minutes, until all of the water is absorbed.

Preheat the grill to high. Thread the tofu on the skewers, creating 8 threaded skewers. Reserve any residual marinade. Place the skewered tofu on the grill and cook for about 20 minutes, turning several times. Pour some of the reserved sauce over the tofu skewers as they grill, reserving the remainder of the sauce to pass at the table.

Remove the skewers from the grill. Spoon equal amounts of rice on 4 warm serving plates and top each with 2 tofu skewers. Drizzle with reserved marinade and serve with Peanut Sauce or Creamy Ponzu Sauce, if desired.

Yield: 4 main-dish servings

Tofu in Garlic-Soy Marinade

INGREDIENTS

28 ounces (800 grams) extra-firm
   tofu

Garlic-Soy Marinade (page 29)

2 medium green bell peppers

1 ½ cups (280 grams) uncooked
   long-grain brown rice

Dilled Yogurt and Sour Cream
   Sauce (page 51)

Try this entrée with Dilled Yogurt and Sour Cream Sauce (page 51) and a salad for a wonderful meal.

Soak 12 wooden skewers in water. Cut the slabs of tofu through the middle to create 4 pieces. Place each piece on a paper towel, cover with another towel, and place a heavy skillet on top to remove excess moisture. After 15 minutes, place the slabs between fresh towels to repeat the process. Cut each slab into 6 pieces to form cubes.

Place the about half of the Garlic-Soy Marinade in a shallow baking dish and add the tofu in a single layer. Pour the remainder of the marinade over the top. Marinate for about an hour, gently turning the pieces after about 30 minutes.

Meanwhile, cut the bell peppers lengthwise from the stem ends and discard the stems, membranes, and seeds. Cut the bell peppers into uniform pieces about 1 inch square. Set aside.

Heat 3 ¼ cups (750 milliliters) water to a boil in a medium saucepan on the stovetop for the rice. Stir in the rice, cover the pan, and reduce the heat to low. Cook for about 40 minutes. Remove from the heat and set aside until needed.

Preheat the grill to high. Using 2 skewers per serving, place them about ½-inch apart and start with a square of bell pepper, threading it on 2 skewers. Alternately thread the tofu and bell pepper, creating 6 threaded skewers. Reserve any residual marinade. Place the skewers on the grill and cook for about 20 minutes, turning several times.

To serve, mound equal amounts of rice on 6 warm serving plates and top each plate with 2 skewers. Drizzle with the reserved marinade. Serve with the Dilled Yogurt and Sour Cream Sauce if desired.

Yield: 6 main-dish servings

Cumin and Coriander Seed-Crusted Tofu

INGREDIENTS

14 ounces (400 grams) extra-firm tofu

1/2 cup (50 grams) cumin seed

1/2 cup (40 grams) coriander seed

2 tablespoons (28 milliliters) sesame oil

6 ounces (170 grams) pepper jack cheese, sliced

2 cups (320 grams) fresh or frozen corn kernels, cooked

Salsa or dipping sauce (optional)

This entrée is flavorful served over the cooked corn as is, but for a real treat, serve it with Smooth Tomatillo Salsa (page 38) or Grilled Red Bell Pepper Mayonnaise (page 47) as well. I've included this recipe in the skewered chapter because the cheese-stuffed slices of tofu are held together with toothpicks even though they cook in a grill basket, tightly enclosing the cheese-stuffed tofu.

Cut the slab of tofu through the middle to create 2 pieces. Place each piece on a paper towel, cover with another towel, and place a heavy skillet on top to remove excess moisture. After 15 minutes, place the slabs between fresh towels to repeat the process. Cut each slab into 4 pieces, then slice the pieces in half through the middle, stacking each of the 8 pieces next to each other.

Grind together the cumin and coriander seeds in a mortar and pestle or in a seed grinder. Place the seeds on a baking sheet or cutting board in an even layer. Brush the outsides of the tofu with the sesame oil. Place the tofu pieces on top of the seeds and press to encrust them. Place an equal amount of pepper jack cheese on half of the pieces and cover with the remaining pieces of tofu as you would when making a sandwich, creating 4 cheese-filled tofu steaks. Secure the halves with toothpicks.

Meanwhile, preheat the grill to medium-low. Place the tofu steaks in the grilling basket and set it on the grill. Grill for 3 minutes, turn carefully, and continue to grill for 3 more minutes.

Mound the cooked corn on 4 warm serving plates and top each serving with a tofu steak, removing the toothpicks before serving. Serve with salsa or dipping sauce if desired.

Yield: 4 main-dish servings

CHAPTER 9
Fajitas, Tacos, Burritos, and Quesadillas

This chapter is full of easy summer meals. Serve them as a hurry-up dinner after work, or showcase several dishes for a fun party. They are easy to prepare, quick to serve, and promise to please your family and guests.

To complete the meal, serve black or refried beans and steamed rice. Season the cooked beans with cumin, coriander, mild chili powder, a fresh bay leaf, and a bit of salt as you gently heat them through. Add some tomato juice and minced serrano chiles to the rice as it cooks to give it a Tex-Mex flair. Turn to "Salsas, Chutneys, and Dipping Sauces," beginning on page 34, and prepare a selection of condiments to serve. If you are in a pinch for time, you may also serve your favorite commercially prepared salsas or sauces. Always set out a basket of your favorite corn chips.

Fajitas are the perfect choice for casual dining. They are easy to prepare and festive to serve. Purchase inexpensive oval fajita pans from a Mexican specialty market or use a baking tray or cast-iron skillet to cook the ingredients on the grill. If using fajita pans, you can transfer them directly to the table, placing the hot pans on tiles or hot-plate holders. If using a baking tray or skillet, transfer the cooked ingredients to a warm serving platter. Serve the Corn, Potato, and Leek Fajitas (page 172) early in the summer, when you can still find tender leeks and fresh corn has just appeared at the market. Allow each diner to create his or her own entrée, customizing it from the ingredients you present. Serve different condiments—salsas and Guacamole (page 48) are a must—to top off the tortilla-encased bundles.

Tacos—either crisp or soft—are a delicious finger food. As with fajitas, diners can assemble their own tacos. All you do is prepare the filling and set out the crisp or soft corn tortillas and an array of condiments. Try the Tacos with Grilled Peppers, Black Beans, and Blue Cheese (page 176) for an easy-to-prepare, casual dinner party. Serve margaritas or ice-cold beer, chips and salsa, and a freshly sliced cantaloupe for a delightful meal.

Burritos are a family favorite, a humble yet flavorful offering. Some of the ingredients are grilled in advance and then mixed with the rest of the filling. Once the burritos are placed on the grill, they cook quickly, so make sure the rest of the meal is ready to serve. Placing a smoker box on the grill yields a flavorful twist to any of these recipes. We think of burritos as a simple meal, but the Refried Bean Burritos with Smoked Gouda and Spicy Tomato Sauce (page 183) or the Burritos with Spinach, Artichokes, Grilled Red Bell Pepper, and Feta Cheese (page 184) elevate this humble fare to gourmet status. Be sure to select fresh, large, burrito-size tortillas for any of these recipes.

Quesadillas are the "grilled cheese sandwich" of Mexican cuisine. Quick and easy to prepare, the simple cheese quesadilla is a favorite standby lunch or light dinner offering. A flour tortilla with cheese is the standard, but adding mango, nopalito cactus, or flavorful mushrooms opens the door to gastronomic delights. Brie and Mango Quesadillas (page 186) are a delicious main course, or they can star as the opening dish for a multi-course grilled meal.

Corn, Potato, and Leek Fajitas

INGREDIENTS

4 ears yellow corn, not husked

2 leeks

$1/4$ teaspoon olive oil

4 red potatoes

2 tablespoons (28 milliliters)
canola oil

$1/4$ cup (60 milliliters) freshly
squeezed lime juice

1 tablespoon (14 milliliters) honey

2 cloves garlic, minced

$1/4$ teaspoon ground cumin

$1/4$ teaspoon ground coriander

$1/4$ teaspoon mild chili powder

2 jalapeño chiles, seeded and
diced

1 large red bell pepper, seeded and
cut into thin strips

12 fajita-size tortillas

Guacamole (page 48) or
prepared guacamole

Salsa Fresca (page 45) or
prepared salsa

When the first summer corn hits the markets, prepare this dish. New red potatoes will still be in season, as will leeks. You must serve these fajitas with Guacamole (page 48) and a salsa such as Salsa Fresca (page 45).

Place the corn in a plastic bag and fill the bag with water to soak the husks for about 15 minutes. Meanwhile, preheat the grill to high. Remove the corn from the bag of water and place the corn on the grill. Turn every few minutes to blacken all sides of the husks evenly. Grill for about 18 to 22 minutes. (The kernels will steam in the husks.) Remove the corn from the grill. Allow the corn to cool for a few minutes, then peel off the husks and remove the silk. Cut the kernels from the cob and set them aside.

While the corn is cooking, trim the root ends and upper green tops from the leeks. Carefully wash the leeks to remove any dirt. Cut the leeks lengthwise and brush with the olive oil. Place the leeks, cut sides down, on the grill and grill for 8 minutes. Set the leeks aside on a cutting board to cool for a few minutes and then cut into thin slices.

Meanwhile, place the potatoes in the microwave on high and cook for about 4 minutes until just soft. (They will finish cooking on the grill.) Remove the potatoes and set aside to cool for several minutes, then cut into bite-size cubes.

In a small bowl, whisk together the canola oil, lime juice, honey, garlic, cumin, coriander, and chili powder. Add the jalapeño chiles and whisk to combine.

Place the leeks, potatoes, and bell pepper in a large bowl and pour the sauce over them. Gently toss to combine. Place 2 fajita pans or a large-cast iron skillet on the grill and add the vegetables. Heat, turning frequently, for about 15 minutes. Wrap the tortillas in foil and place on a cool spot on the grill to heat through.

Transfer the vegetables and tortillas to the table and serve. Pass your favorite guacamole and salsa.

Yield: 6 main-dish servings

Chile, Crookneck Squash,
and Onion Fajitas with Queso Fresco

INGREDIENTS

¹/₄ cup (60 milliliters) olive oil

¹/₄ cup (60 milliliters) freshly
   squeezed lime juice

2 cloves minced garlic

¹/₄ teaspoon ground cumin

¹/₄ teaspoon ground coriander

¹/₄ teaspoon mild chili powder

6 mild Anaheim chiles

1 pound (455 grams) yellow
   crookneck squash

2 yellow onions

12 fajita-size tortillas

¹/₂ pound (225 grams)
   crumbled queso fresco

Salsa Fresca (page 45) or
   prepared salsa

Guacamole (page 48) or
   prepared guacamole

Sour cream

This fajita is colorful and flavorful, and the yellow crooknecks add a taste of summer. Many varieties of long green chiles are available. I like Anaheim chiles, but you can prepare this dish with any mild or hot chile, depending on your taste. Pass Salsa Fresca (page 45), Guacamole (page 48), and sour cream.

In a small bowl, whisk together the olive oil, lime juice, garlic, cumin, coriander, and chili powder. Set aside. Preheat the grill to high.

Remove and discard the stems of the Anaheim chiles and scrape out the seeds for a milder dish. Cut the chiles into long strips.

Trim and discard the ends from the squashes and cut them into thick matchsticks.

Peel the onions and cut them in half. Slice the halves and separate the rings. Put the chiles, squashes, and onions in a plastic bag and drizzle with the olive-oil mixture.

Place 2 fajita pans or a large cast-iron skillet on the grill and add the vegetables from the bag, drizzling all of the oil mixture over them. Heat, turning frequently, for about 15 minutes. Wrap the tortillas in foil and place on a cool spot on the grill to heat through.

Transfer the vegetables and tortillas to the table and serve. Pass the queso fresco, salsa, guacamole, and sour cream.

Yield: 6 main-dish servings

Fajitas with Grilled Summer Squash,
Refried Beans, and Fresh Squash Blossoms

INGREDIENTS

1/4 cup (60 milliliters) canola oil

1/4 cup (60 milliliters) freshly squeezed lime juice

6 teaspoons minced oregano

6 assorted small summer squashes

2 white onions, sliced

12 fresh squash blossoms, stems trimmed to about 1 inch

12 fajita-size tortillas

15 ounces (430 grams) canned vegetarian refried beans

1 teaspoon crushed garlic

1/2 teaspoon cumin

1/2 teaspoon mild chili powder

1/4 teaspoon salt

8 ounces (225 grams) grated Monterey Jack cheese

1 cup (240 g) Mexican Crema (page 48)

1 cup Salsa Fresca (page 45)

The colorful ingredients in this recipe come together to create a delicious fajita. Harvest squash blossoms early in the morning from your garden, beg some from a gardening neighbor, or purchase them at the farmers' market.

In a small bowl, whisk together the canola oil, lime juice, and oregano. Set aside. Preheat the grill to high.

Trim the ends from the squashes and cut them into thick matchsticks. Peel the onions and cut them in half. Slice the halves and separate the rings. Put the squashes and onions in a plastic bag and drizzle with the canola-oil mixture.

Place 2 fajita pans or a large cast-iron skillet on the grill and add the squashes and onions from the bag, drizzling the oil mixture remaining in the bag over them. Heat, turning frequently, for about 15 minutes. Add the squash blossoms right before you remove the fajita pans from the grill.

While the vegetables are cooking, wrap the tortillas in foil and place on a cool spot on the grill to heat through.

Meanwhile, place the refried beans in a saucepan with 1/4 cup (60 milliliters) water. Add the garlic, cumin, chili powder, and salt. Heat the beans over medium-low, stirring occasionally. Transfer to a serving bowl and keep warm.

Transfer the squashes and onions and tortillas to the table. Pass the refried beans, Monterey Jack cheese, Mexican Crema, and Salsa Fresca. Allow the diners to assemble their own fajitas.

Yield: 6 main-dish servings

Tacos with Grilled Peppers,
Black Beans, and Blue Cheese

INGREDIENTS

1 large red bell pepper

1 large yellow bell pepper

2 ripe Haas avocados

2 tablespoons (28 milliliters)
   freshly squeezed lime juice

15 ounces (430 grams) canned
   black beans

4 green onions, diced

1/4 teaspoon ground cumin

1/4 teaspoon ground coriander

1/2 teaspoon mild chili powder

2 ounces (55 grams) crumbled
   blue cheese

6 teaspoons minced fresh oregano

12 standard-size corn tortillas

2 cups (140 grams) finely
   shredded green cabbage

These soft tacos are fun to serve at a small dinner party. The guests can assemble their own—all you do is prepare the ingredients and set the table. Serve with steamed rice and Smooth Tomatillo Salsa (page 38). Save any leftovers and use them as an omelet filling the following morning. Haas avocados have pebbled dark green or black skins.

Preheat the grill to high. Place the bell peppers directly on the grill and cook for 10 to 15 minutes, turning frequently. Cook until the skins are charred black. Transfer the peppers to a plastic or paper bag, close the bag, and set aside for about 15 minutes. When the peppers are cool enough to handle, peel off the charred skin, discard the seeds, stems, and white membranes, and cut into narrow strips. Place the strips in a bowl.

Cut the avocados in half lengthwise and remove the pits. With the avocados still in the skin, use the tip of a sharp knife to cut into cubes. Use a spoon to scoop the cubes into the bowl with the peppers. Drizzle with the lime juice and toss gently to combine. Add the black beans and green onions and toss again.

Combine the cumin, coriander, and chili powder in a small bowl and sprinkle over the pepper mixture. Toss to combine. Crumble the blue cheese and oregano over the pepper mixture and toss well to combine.

Place the tortillas in foil and warm them on the grill. Transfer the pepper mixture, tortillas, and green cabbage to the table and allow diners to fill their own tacos.

Yield: 6 main-dish servings

Soft Tacos with
Grilled Tofu and Pickled Jalapeños

INGREDIENTS

14 ounces (400 grams) extra-firm tofu

3 tablespoons (45 milliliters) canola oil

1 medium yellow onion, diced

2 cloves garlic, minced

1 teaspoon ground cumin

1 teaspoon mild chili powder

1 teaspoon minced fresh oregano

$1/8$ teaspoon black pepper

$3/4$ cup (185 grams) tomato sauce

3 teaspoons minced pickled jalapeño chiles

2 medium tomatoes, diced

12 corn tortillas

2 cups (140 grams) finely shredded green cabbage

Serve these delicious tacos accompanied by Peach and Pineapple Salsa with Fresh Tarragon (page 42) and Mexican Crema (page 48) for a real taste treat. If time is tight, serve with your favorite commercially prepared salsa and sour cream.

Preheat the grill to medium-high with a smoker box in place. Drain the tofu and cut the slabs in half width-wise. Place the tofu on a paper towel, cover with another paper towel, and weigh down with a heavy skillet to press out most of the moisture. Again, cut the slabs in half width-wise and brush each side with 1 tablespoon of the canola oil. Place the tofu on a grill tray and then on the hot grill. Grill for about 10 minutes, turning several times. Remove the tofu from the grill and set aside to cool slightly.

Meanwhile, place the remaining 2 tablespoons canola oil in a cast-iron skillet over medium-high heat on the stovetop and add the onion, garlic, cumin, chili powder, oregano, and black pepper. Sauté for about 2 minutes, then add the tomato sauce and jalapeño chiles. Crumble the grilled tofu and add to the skillet. Stir to incorporate and continue to cook for about 5 minutes.

Place the tortillas in foil and warm them on the grill. Transfer the tofu mixture, tortillas, and green cabbage to the table and allow diners to fill their own tacos.

Yield: 6 main-dish servings

Grilled Tomatillo
and Potato Tacos with Jack Cheese

INGREDIENTS

1½ pounds (700 grams) tomatillos, in the husk

1 pound (455 grams) red potatoes

2 poblano chiles, seeded and chopped

¼ cup (60 milliliters) canola oil

1 teaspoon mild chili powder

½ teaspoon cumin

½ teaspoon salt

8 ounces (225 grams) grated Monterey Jack cheese

2 cups (140 grams) finely shredded green cabbage

1 cup (60 grams) Mexican Crema (page 48)

12 crisp taco shells

These tacos are brimming with flavor and are a visual delight. Serve Guacamole (page 48), salsa, and chips as an appetizer, with White Corn with Chili Butter (page 96), to complete the meal. Prepare fresh Mexican Crema (page 48) or use a commercially prepared variety. You can also substitute sour cream if you wish.

Place the tomatillos, still in their husks, in a plastic bag and fill the bag with water. Seal and allow the tomatillos to soak for about 15 minutes.

Preheat the grill to high with a smoker box in place. Remove the tomatillos from the bag and place them on the grill. Grill for 15 to 18 minutes, turning frequently. (The husks will char slightly, but should not totally blacken.) Remove the husks and chop the tomatillos. Set aside in a bowl.

Meanwhile, cut the red potatoes into cubes and place them, along with the poblano chiles, in a plastic bag.

In a small bowl, whisk together the canola oil, chili powder, cumin, and salt. Drizzle over the potatoes and poblano chiles. Seal the bag, allowing some of the air to remain. Toss gently to coat the potatoes and poblano chiles evenly.

Place 2 fajita pans or a cast-iron skillet on the grill and add the potatoes mixture from the bag. Cook for 8 to 10 minutes, turning frequently. Add the tomatillos and toss to combine.

Place the tomatillo mixture, Monterey Jack cheese, green cabbage, Mexican Crema, and taco shells on the table and allow diners to fill their own tacos.

Yield: 6 main-dish servings

Black Bean and
Jack Cheese Burritos

INGREDIENTS

14 ounces (400 grams) canned black beans

$1/2$ teaspoon crushed garlic

$1/4$ teaspoon ground cumin

$1/4$ teaspoon ground coriander

$1/4$ teaspoon salt

1 jalapeño chile, seeded and minced

4 burrito-size flour tortillas

8 ounces (225 grams) grated Monterey Jack cheese

2 tablespoons (28 milliliters) canola oil

1 avocado, seeded, peeled, and sliced

Salsa Fresca (page 45)

Corn chips

The flavorful black beans and melted jack cheese in this recipe make an outstanding burrito. Serve with corn chips and Salsa Fresca (page 45).

Drain the black beans, reserving about 2 tablespoons of the liquid. Place the beans in a blender with the reserved liquid, garlic, cumin, coriander, salt, and jalapeño chile. Puree until chunky-smooth.

Preheat the grill to medium-high. Working with one tortilla at a time, place one-quarter of the beans slightly off-center and top with one-quarter of the cheese. Fold up the bottom end, then roll the sides to close. Set aside, seam side down.

Place 2 fajita pans or a large cast-iron skillet or baking tray directly on the grill and coat with the oil. Place the burritos on the pans, skillet, or tray, seam sides down. Cook for about 3 minutes, turn, and continue to cook for 3 minutes until nicely browned on each side. Top with the avocado and serve immediately, passing Salsa Fresca and corn chips.

Yield: 4 main-dish servings

Grilled Vegetable
and Rice Burritos

INGREDIENTS

¹/₂ cup (90 grams) uncooked
long-grain brown rice

2 medium yellow onions

2 tablespoons (28 milliliters)
olive oil

3 medium zucchini

2 red bell peppers

6 burrito-size flour tortillas

2 tablespoons (28 milliliters)
freshly squeezed lime juice

1 tablespoon (14 milliliters)
canola oil

1 teaspoon minced chipotle
chiles in adobo

1¹/₂ cups (100 grams) shredded
red cabbage

The grilled vegetables and chipotle chile lend a delicate smoky flavor to this dish. Chipotle chiles in adobo are sold in most supermarkets and all Mexican specialty stores. If you like things spicy, double the amount of chipotle chiles.

Bring 1 cup (235 milliliters) water to a boil in a small saucepan. Add the rice and return to a boil. Reduce the heat to very low, cover the pan, and cook for 45 minutes. Remove the saucepan from the heat and set aside, leaving the lid in place.

Meanwhile, preheat the grill to high with a smoker box in place. Trim off and discard the ends of the onions and peel them. Cut the onions in half crosswise and lightly brush the cut sides with some of the olive oil. Place the onions on the grill, cut sides down. Cover the grill and grill for about 35 minutes, turning every 8 to 10 minutes. (The onions are done when they are soft and slightly charred.)

While the onions are cooking, remove and discard the ends from the zucchini and cut them lengthwise into 3 strips. Cut the bell peppers in half, discard the stems, seeds, and white membranes, and then slice each half into thirds lengthwise. Place the zucchini and bell peppers in a plastic bag and drizzle with the remaining olive oil. Twist the bag to seal, allowing some air to remain in the bag. Toss gently to coat the vegetables evenly. Remove the zucchini and peppers from the bag, place on the grill, and grill for 15 to 20 minutes, turning several times while cooking. (They will char slightly and become limp.)

While the vegetables are cooking, wrap the tortillas in foil and place them on a cool spot on the grill to heat through.

Remove all of the vegetables from the grill and allow them to cool slightly, then coarsely chop them. Place the vegetables in a medium bowl and add the rice. Toss to combine. Add the lime juice, canola oil, and chipotle chiles to the bowl and toss to combine.

Just before serving, lay the tortillas flat on individual warmed serving plates. Evenly divide the grilled vegetable mixture and cabbage among the tortillas. Fold the ends of each tortilla over the filling and roll closed. Serve immediately.

Yield: 6 main-dish servings

Refried Bean Burritos
with Smoked Gouda and Spicy Tomato Sauce

INGREDIENTS

15 ounces (430 grams) canned
   refried beans

$1/2$ cup (115 grams) sour cream

1 teaspoon mild chili powder

$1/4$ teaspoon cumin

$1/4$ teaspoon coriander

$1/4$ teaspoon salt

6 burrito-size flour tortillas

8 ounces (225 grams) shredded
   smoked Gouda cheese

2 tablespoons (28 milliliters)
   canola oil

2 tablespoons (30 grams) spicy
   tomato sauce

Mexican Crema (page 48) or sour
   cream (optional)

This is a fast and easy burrito to prepare, since it calls for commercially prepared spicy tomato sauce or enchilada sauce. There are many varieties available, especially in Mexican specialty markets.

Place the refried beans in a blender or food processor with the sour cream and $1/8$ to $1/4$ cup (30 to 60 milliliters) water. Pulse to combine. Add the chili powder, cumin, coriander, and salt. Puree until blended to a thick (but not watery) consistency.

Preheat the grill to medium-high. Working with one tortilla at a time, place one-sixth of the beans slightly off-center and top with one-sixth of the cheese. Fold up the bottom end, then roll the sides to close. Set aside, seam side down.

Place 2 fajita pans or a large cast-iron skillet or baking tray directly on the grill and coat with the canola oil. Place the burritos on the pans, skillet, or tray, seam sides down. Cook for about 3 minutes, turn, and continue to cook for 3 minutes, until nicely browned on each side. Brush the sauce evenly over the burritos, turn, and continue to cook for a minute or so. Serve the burritos immediately, passing Mexican Crema (page 48) or sour cream, if desired.

Yield: 6 main-dish servings

Burritos with Spinach,
Artichokes, Grilled Red Bell Pepper, and Feta Cheese

INGREDIENTS

1 large red bell pepper

1/2 cup (90 grams) uncooked long-grain white rice

1/4 cup (15 grams) minced fresh flat-leaf parsley

1 tablespoon (14 milliliters) olive oil

6 ounces (170 grams) jarred water-packed artichoke hearts

1 1/2 pounds (700 grams) fresh spinach

3 teaspoons minced fresh marjoram leaves

6 burrito-size flour tortillas, at room temperature

4 ounces (115 grams) crumbled feta cheese

2 tablespoons (28 milliliters) canola oil

These burritos have an unconventional filling that yields a delicious dish. Serve with a salad and some chips and salsa.

Preheat the grill to high. Place the bell pepper directly on the grill and grill for 10 to 15 minutes, turning frequently. (The skin will be charred black.) Transfer the pepper to a plastic bag, close the bag, and set aside for about 15 minutes. When the pepper is cool enough to handle, peel off the charred skin and discard the seeds, stems, and white membrane. Dice the pepper and set aside.

Bring 1 cup (235 milliliters) water to a boil in a medium saucepan on the stovetop. Stir in the white rice, parsley, and olive oil. Cover, reduce the heat to very low, and cook 20 minutes. Remove the saucepan from the heat and set aside, leaving the lid in place.

Drain the artichoke hearts and cut them into bite-size pieces.

Carefully wash the spinach, discarding the stems. Pile the spinach into a saucepan, place on the stovetop, cover, and cook over medium heat until the spinach wilts, about 5 minutes. Drain the spinach in a colander, pressing with a wooden spoon to remove as much water as possible. Transfer the spinach to a cutting board and coarsely chop. Return the spinach to the warm saucepan, along with the artichoke hearts, grilled bell pepper, marjoram, and cooked rice. Stir to combine.

Working with one tortilla at a time, place one-sixth of the spinach mixture slightly off-center and top with one-sixth of the cheese. Fold up the bottom end, then roll the sides to close. Set aside, seam side down.

Place 2 fajita pans or a large cast-iron skillet or baking tray on the grill and coat with the canola oil. Place the burritos on the pans, skillet, or tray, seam sides down. Cook for about 3 minutes, turn, and continue to cook for 3 minutes, until nicely browned on each side. Serve immediately.

Yield: 6 main-dish servings

Mushroom and Cheese Quesadillas

INGREDIENTS

1 medium serrano chile

$^1/_2$ teaspoon cumin seed

$^1/_2$ pound (225 grams) button
mushrooms

$^1/_2$ medium white onion, sliced

$^1/_4$ teaspoon salt

$^1/_2$ cup Vegetable Stock (page 25)

1 tablespoon (14 milliliters)
dry sherry

4 standard-size flour tortillas

4 ounces (115 grams) shredded mild
cheddar cheese

Salsa (optional)

Mexican Crema (page 48)
(optional)

This flavorful mushroom mixture is delicious melted with cheese in quesadillas. Serve with Smooth Tomatillo Salsa (page 38) and Mexican Crema (page 48) or your favorite salsa.

Remove and discard the stems of the serrano chile; scrape out the seeds and membrane for a milder dish. Finely mince the chile and set aside.

Crush the cumin with a mortar and pestle. Set aside.

Brush or wipe any loose dirt particles from the mushrooms and thinly slice them.

Place the mushrooms, onion, serrano chile, and cumin in a skillet or sauté pan that has a tight-fitting lid. Sprinkle with the salt and pour in the Vegetable Stock. Place the skillet on the stovetop, cover, and cook over medium heat for 10 minutes. Remove the lid, and continue to stir and cook if more than a tablespoon of liquid remains in the pan. When the mixture is fairly dry, turn off the heat and stir in the sherry. Set aside.

Meanwhile, preheat the grill to medium-high. Place the tortillas on a work surface and distribute one-eighth of the cheese on half of each tortilla. Distribute the mushroom mixture equally over the cheese on each tortilla, then top the mushrooms with the remaining cheese. Fold the tortillas in half, enclosing the filling. Place the quesadillas directly on the grill and grill for about 8 minutes, carefully turning several times so the cheese melts and the tortillas get grill marks but do not burn. Serve immediately, passing salsa and Mexican Crema (page 48), if desired.

Yield: 4 main-dish servings

Brie and Mango Quesadillas

INGREDIENTS

4 standard-size flour tortillas

$1/2$ pound (225 grams) brie, thinly
   sliced

I ripe mango, peeled, pitted, and
   chopped

Mango and Papaya Salsa with
   Jalapeños (page 37) or
   prepared salsa

*This may sound like an unusual combination, but the flavors combine
to create a delicious quesadilla. This is also a tasty appetizer for eight
people. Serve with Mango and Papaya Salsa with Jalapeños (page 37).*

Preheat the grill to medium-high. Lie the tortillas on a work surface. Place several slices of brie on half of each tortilla. Top with
equal amounts of mango. Place the remaining slices of brie over
the mango and fold the tortilla in half, enclosing the filling. Place
the quesadillas directly on the grill and grill for about 8 minutes,
carefully turning several times so the cheese melts and the tortillas
get grill marks but do not burn. Serve immediately with Mango
and Papaya Salsa with Jalapeños or prepared salsa.

Yield: 4 main-dish servings

Nopalito and Tomato Quesadillas

INGREDIENTS

1/2 pound (225 grams) fresh
nopales

2 pear tomatoes

I large poblano chile

I teaspoon cumin seed

I tablespoon (28 milliliters)
canola oil

2 green onions, minced

I clove garlic, minced

1/2 teaspoon salt

6 standard-size flour tortillas

6 ounces (170 grams)
crumbled queso fresco

Salsa Fresca (page 45)

When they are cut, raw prickly pear cactus paddles—nopales—have a slimy quality similar to that of okra. This cooks away to yield a flavor that is a cross between lime and green beans. You can find nopales at gourmet shops and Mexican specialty groceries. Serve these quesadillas with White Corn with Chili Butter (page 96) for a delightful meal.

The thorns of the nopales, which are lodged under the small bumps that irregularly dot the paddles, usually have been shaved off by the grower. If not, use the dull edge of a knife blade to scrape off the thorns, taking care not to stick yourself. Do not remove the peel, however. Lay the nopales flat on a work surface and then cut off and discard 1/2 inch of the outer rim and the base end. Slice the paddles lengthwise into 1/4-inch strips, then cut the strips into 1-inch pieces. Place the nopales in a saucepan and cover with water. Bring to a boil on the stovetop, reduce the heat to medium-high, cover the pan, and cook for about 15 minutes, until fork-tender. Drain the nopales in a colander and rinse well with cold water. Pat dry with paper towels and set aside.

Meanwhile, chop the tomatoes and place in a bowl. Remove and discard the stem, seeds, and membrane from the poblano chile. Finely dice it and add to the bowl. Add the cooked nopales and toss to combine.

Crush the cumin with a mortar and pestle.

Heat the canola oil over medium heat in a heavy skillet. Stir in the cumin, green onions, and garlic and sauté for 1 to 2 minutes. Add the tomato mixture and the salt. Increase the heat to medium-high and cook, stirring occasionally, for about 10 minutes, until all the liquid has evaporated.

Preheat the grill to medium-high. Place the tortillas on a work surface. Distribute equal amounts of the tomato mixture on half of each tortilla. Sprinkle with equal amounts of the queso fresco and fold the tortillas in half, enclosing the filling. Place the quesadillas directly on the grill and grill for about 8 minutes, carefully turning several times so the cheese melts and the tortillas get grill marks but do not burn. Serve immediately with Salsa Fresca (page 45).

Yield: 6 main-dish servings

CHAPTER 10

Wraps, Sandwiches, and Burgers

We all need convenience foods that we can quickly prepare, take for lunch, or eat on the run. The recipes in this chapter fit that bill. There are many variations of the wrap, sandwich, or burger, but all have one thing in common: Tasty ingredients are encased in leavened or flat bread and presented to eat without a fork or knife. These stuffed or layered casual meals are sometimes messy, but they're always satisfying.

Wraps are easy to make and transport well—they are the perfect meal-on-the-go. Most of the filling ingredients can be prepared ahead of time, and then encased in the wrap when ready to serve or to pack as a weekday lunch. Wraps make a delicious lunch or light supper. The Lovash with Grilled Peppers and Eggplant (page 192) is a great recipe to serve as part of a buffet, or to take to a party. The pinwheel slices are easy to eat and transport well. Tightly wrap any leftovers and refrigerate them to be enjoyed the next day.

Everyone loves a sandwich, and adding grilled ingredients or grilling the whole thing makes the everyday sandwich even more delicious. Grilled Tomato and Cheese Sandwiches (page 194) or Grilled Cheese Sandwiches with Cremini Mushrooms (page 201) are simple to prepare but worthy of gourmet status. Focaccia buns are the perfect shape for grilled portobello mushrooms or grilled eggplant. Invite some friends over mid-week for Grilled Eggplant on Focaccia (page 196) or Focaccia with Grilled Portobello Mushrooms (page 195) for an easy but delicious grilled dinner. Serve with a simple salad and chilled wine and dine alfresco.

The burger is revered; there is something universal about putting a grilled patty of some sort on a bun with lettuce and tomato slices. Pass your favorite mustards and mayonnaise. Add sweet or tart pickles or relish and enjoy! The Grilled Tempeh Burgers (page 202) are certain to become a family favorite.

Anaheim Chile
and Curry Tofu Wrap

INGREDIENTS

6 Anaheim chiles

6 chapatis or whole wheat tortillas

14 ounces (400 grams) firm tofu

3 green onions, minced

1/3 cup (80 grams) mayonnaise

1/4 cup (4 grams) minced fresh
   cilantro

2 teaspoons curry powder

2 teaspoons freshly squeezed
   lime juice

1/4 teaspoon salt

Tofu will take on any flavor, and pairing it with curry spices is a great combination. Serve this with sliced raw vegetables for a nice lunch or serve with cucumber salad and Summer Squashes with Lemon Basil (page 93) as a dinner entrée.

Preheat the grill to high. Place the Anaheim chiles on the grill and grill for 8 to 10 minutes, turning frequently. (The skins will blacken.) Remove the chiles from the grill and place in a plastic bag. Seal the bag and set aside to cool. When the chiles are cool enough to handle, remove the blackened skin and place the chiles lengthwise on a cutting board, removing and discarding the stem end and seeds. Set the chiles aside.

Wrap the chapatis (a type of Indian flat bread) or tortillas in foil and place on the cooling grill for about 10 minutes, leaving them there until needed so they stay warm.

Meanwhile, cut the tofu into 1/2-inch slices and place the slices on a paper towel and cover with another towel. Place a heavy skillet on top to press the excess water from the tofu. After 15 minutes, place the tofu slices between fresh towels and repeat the process. Crumble the tofu into a bowl. Mix in the green onions, mayonnaise, cilantro, curry powder, lime juice, and salt.

Place a warm chapati or tortilla on a work surface and place one chile just off center on the bread. Use a spoon to mound one-sixth of the tofu mixture on top of the chile. Fold up the bottom and fold in the sides, then roll up tightly. Fill the remaining chapatis or tortillas in the same manner. Serve immediately or individually wrap tightly in plastic or waxed paper to enjoy later.

Yield: 6 main-dish servings

INGREDIENTS

2 medium eggplants

2 tablespoons (30 grams) coarse salt

1/4 cup (60 milliliters) olive oil

4 large red bell peppers

I pound (455 grams) cream cheese, at room temperature

I cup Basil Pesto (page 23)

3 tablespoons (45 milliliters) freshly squeezed lemon juice

3 rounds fresh lovash bread or crisp rounds, softened

I cup (100 grams) pitted and chopped kalamata olives

8 cups (240 grams) baby spinach leaves

Lovash is Armenian cracker bread, most commonly sold with three large crisp rounds to a package. Follow the manufacturer's directions to soften the crisp rounds. You may find soft rounds in the refrigerator section of some ethnic or natural food stores. This recipe is a great one to make ahead of time to serve as part of the meal for a small gathering of friends. Served as an appetizer, figure about 22 to 24 servings. This can be prepared 1 day ahead.

Preheat the grill to medium-high. Cut off and discard the stem and bottom ends of the eggplants but do not peel them. Cut the eggplants crosswise into slices about 1/2-inch thick. To remove the eggplants' bitter juices, sprinkle both sides of the slices with the salt and place the slices on a rack to for about 30 minutes. (The salt will cause the eggplant to "sweat" and release the bitter juices.) Rinse the eggplant slices briefly and blot them dry with paper towels.

Brush each side of the eggplant slices with the olive oil and place them on the grill. Grill for 5 to 8 minutes until browned, turn, and continue to grill for another 5 to 8 minutes. (The slices should be tender-crisp, not mushy.) Remove the eggplant from the grill and set aside. When the eggplant is cool enough to handle, peel the off the skin from each slice.

Meanwhile, place the bell peppers directly on the grill and grill for 10 to 15 minutes, turning frequently. (The pepper skin will be charred black.) Transfer the peppers to a plastic bag, close the bag, and set aside for about 15 minutes. When the peppers are cool enough to handle, peel off the charred skins and discard the seeds, stems, and white membrane. Cut the peppers into long thin strips and set aside.

Place the cream cheese, Basil Pesto, and lemon juice in a food processor. Pulse to combine.

Working with one round at a time, place the lovash bread on a work surface and spread one-third of the cream cheese mixture evenly over the surface with a spatula, leaving about a 4-inch rim on one edge. Cover with one-third of the eggplant and bell pepper slices. Evenly distribute one-third of the kalamata olives over the eggplant and bell peppers. Cover with one-third of the spinach leaves. Begin at the end covered with the filling and tightly roll up the lovash bread toward the uncovered edge. (The filling will move forward slightly as you roll, filling the 4-inch rim.) Wrap the rolls in plastic or waxed paper, seam sides down, and refrigerate for several hours. Repeat with the remaining lovash bread and ingredients.

Before serving, remove the plastic or waxed paper and slice the rolls into 1-inch rounds. Arrange on a platter and serve.

Yield: 14 main-dish servings

Grilled Tomato and Cheese Sandwiches

INGREDIENTS

2 medium tomatoes

8 slices whole wheat bread

12 ounces (340 grams) sliced mozzarella cheese

I cup (40 grams) loosely packed chiffonaded basil (see page 16 for this technique)

2 tablespoons (28 grams) butter, melted

This sandwich is best prepared in the summer, when fresh garden tomatoes are at their peak. You will have a few more slices of tomatoes than you need for the sandwiches, so use them to garnish the serving plates.

Preheat the grill to medium. Core the tomatoes and slice them into $1/4$-inch slices.

Place the bread on a work surface. Cover each slice with equal amounts of mozzarella cheese. Top half of them with equal amounts of tomato and sprinkle with the basil. Top with the other cheese-covered slices of bread, cheeses side down. Use a pastry brush to lightly coat the outer sides of the bread with the butter. Place the sandwiches on the grill and grill for 4 to 5 minutes, then turn and grill for 3 to 4 more minutes. Slice in half and serve immediately.

Yield: 4 main-dish servings

Grilled Artichoke Panini

INGREDIENTS

I soft-crusted baguette or 4 soft rolls

$1/2$ pound (225 grams) Provolone cheese, sliced

6 ounces (170 grams) jarred marinated artichoke hearts, drained and sliced

$1/2$ cup (50 grams) chopped kalamata olives

4 pepperoncini peppers, sliced

24 basil leaves

The ingredients remind me of Italy, hence the name. Serve a crisp white wine for a casual lunch with friends while you dream of travel plans.

Preheat the grill to medium-high. Cut the baguette into 4 equal pieces and slice each in half, or, if using soft rolls, slice them in half. On the bottom of each slice, place one-eighth of the Provolone cheese and equal amounts of the artichoke hearts, kalamata olives, pepperoncini peppers, and basil leaves. Top with equal amounts of the remaining cheese and cover with the top of the baguette or roll. Place the sandwiches in a grill basket, clamp it closed, and place directly on the grill. Grill for 2 to 3 minutes, turn, and grill for 2 to 3 more minutes. (The cheese will melt and the baguette or rolls will be lightly toasted.) Serve immediately.

Yield: 4 main-dish servings

Focaccia with
Grilled Portobello Mushrooms

This has become a classic vegetarian "burger," and rightly so. It is delicious! You may serve this tasty mushroom on a whole wheat bun, if you prefer.

INGREDIENTS

4 large portobello mushrooms

$1/4$ cup (60 milliliters) olive oil

2 teaspoons crushed garlic

Pinch salt

4 focaccia buns

4 butter lettuce leaves

$1/2$ cup Grilled Red Bell Pepper
   Mayonnaise (page 47)

Trim the stem end from each mushroom so it is flush with the gills.

Whisk together the olive oil, garlic, and salt in a small bowl. Brush the bottom of the mushrooms with some of the oil mixture, then place the mushrooms on a platter, gill sides up. Pour equal amounts of the oil mixture into the gills of each mushroom. Use a pastry brush to distribute the garlic throughout the gills, as some of it will settle in the bottom of the bowl. Set the mushrooms aside for about 15 minutes to let them absorb the oil and garlic.

Meanwhile, preheat the grill to high, then reduce the heat to medium-high. Place the mushrooms on the grill, bottom sides down. Grill for about 10 minutes, then turn and continue to grill for about 10 more minutes.

Slice the focaccia buns in half and place them cut sides down on the grill to toast for a minute or two.

To serve, place the focaccia buns on individual plates and top each one with a mushroom and lettuce leaf. Pass the Grilled Red Bell Pepper Mayonnaise.

Yield: 4 main-dish servings

Grilled Eggplant
on Focaccia

Eggplant develops a wonderful flavor when grilled. I like this on a focaccia bun, but you may use a whole wheat or sourdough bun. The Remoulade Sauce really makes this a spectacular sandwich.

INGREDIENTS

I medium eggplant

I tablespoon (15 grams)
   coarse salt

2 large tomatoes, cored and sliced

2 tablespoons (28 milliliters)
   olive oil

4 focaccia buns

4 butter lettuce leaves

¹/₂ cup Remoulade Sauce
   (page 53)

Cut off and discard the stem and bottom ends of the eggplant and slice the eggplant crosswise into 4 slices about 1-inch thick. To remove the eggplant's bitter juices, sprinkle both sides of the slices with the salt and place them on a rack for about 30 minutes. (The salt will cause the eggplant to "sweat" and release the bitter juices.) Briefly rinse the slices and blot them dry with paper towels.

Remove and discard the stem ends from the tomatoes and cut them into 8 thick slices. Set aside.

Meanwhile, preheat the grill to medium-high. Brush each side of the eggplant slices with the olive oil and place them on the grill. Grill for 7 to 9 minutes until browned, turn, and continue to grill for another 7 to 9 minutes.

Slice the focaccia buns in half and place them cut sides down on the grill to toast for a minute or two.

To serve, place the focaccia buns on individual plates and top each one with an eggplant slice and tomato slices. Top with a lettuce leaf. Pass the Remoulade Sauce.

Yield: 4 main-dish servings

Japanese Eggplant
and Red Bell Pepper Sandwich with Pesto

INGREDIENTS

2 medium red bell peppers

2 Japanese eggplants

3 tablespoons (45 milliliters) olive oil

4 sweet rolls

3/4 cup Basil Pesto (page 23) or prepared pesto

I medium tomato, sliced

2 ounces (55 grams) thinly shaved Parmesan cheese

All of the ingredients for this sandwich are at the peak of the season during the summer. Prepare fresh Basil Pesto (page 23) or use a commercially prepared pesto. Enjoy this sandwich for lunch or for a casual dinner served with a salad.

Preheat the grill to medium-high. Cut the bell peppers in half lengthwise, discarding the stems, seeds, and white membrane. Cut each half in two to create 8 slices. Set aside.

Remove and discard the stem end from the eggplants and cut them lengthwise into 1/4-inch strips. Place the eggplants in a plastic bag with the olive oil and toss to coat evenly.

Place the bell peppers on the grill and grill for about 5 minutes per side until they soften but do not char, turning frequently. Remove the peppers from the grill and set aside. Remove the eggplant from the bag, place on the grill, and cook for about 2 minutes per side. (The eggplant will soften and get grill marks but should not char.)

Slice the sweet rolls in half and coat each side with equal amounts of Basil Pesto or prepared pesto. Layer an equal amount of the grilled bell pepper and eggplant on the bottom side of each bun. Add the tomato and Parmesan cheese, then cover with the top of the bun. Place the sandwiches in a grill basket and heat through for about 2 minutes, turning once. Serve immediately.

Yield: 4 main-course servings

Sweet Rolls
with Grilled Peppers and Endive

INGREDIENTS

I large bulb garlic

¼ teaspoon olive oil

2 medium red bell peppers

2 Anaheim chiles

4 sweet rolls

¼ cup Grilled Red Bell Pepper
Mayonnaise (page 47)

8 slices Monterey Jack cheese

2 small Belgium endives,
separated into leaves

8 marinated sun-dried tomatoes

This is a delightful summertime sandwich, quick to prepare on the grill. You may also duplicate it during the winter months if you live in an area where a variety of fresh peppers are available, by grilling the produce on an indoor grill.

Preheat the grill to medium. Rub the papery skin from the garlic, but do not break into individual cloves. Cut about ¹/₂ inch off the pointed top end of the bulb and rub the cut surface with the olive oil. Place the garlic, cut side up, in a covered clay or glass baking dish and place on the grill. (You can wrap it in foil. Then place the foil packet on a baking stone or on baking bricks so the garlic cooks but does not burn on the bottom.) Grill the garlic for about 45 minutes. When the garlic feels very soft when gently squeezed, remove from the grill. Set aside and cool for several minutes. When the garlic is cool enough to handle, squeeze the garlic paste from the cloves into a small bowl.

Cut the bell peppers in half lengthwise, discarding the stems, seeds, and white membrane. Cut each half in two to create 8 slices.

Cut each Anaheim chile from the stem to create 8 slices, discarding the stems and seeds. Place the bell peppers and Anaheim chiles on the grill and grill for about 2 minutes per side, until they soften but do not char. Remove the peppers and chiles from the grill and set aside.

Slice the sweet rolls in half. Spread the grilled garlic evenly on the bottom side of each roll. Apply the Grilled Red Bell Pepper Mayonnaise to the top sides. Layer the Monterey Jack cheese, grilled bell peppers, grilled Anaheim chiles, endive, and sun-dried tomatoes on the garlic side of the roll. Cover with the top of the roll and serve.

Yield: 4 main-dish servings

WRAPS, SANDWICHES, AND BURGERS ☀ 199

Tofu "BLT" Sandwich

INGREDIENTS

14 ounces (400 grams) extra-firm
   tofu

2 tablespoons (28 milliliters)
   toasted sesame oil

12 slices sourdough bread

2 tablespoons (28 grams) butter,
   melted

1/4 cup (120 grams) mayonnaise

2 tablespoons (30 grams) Dijon
   mustard

3 medium tomatoes, thinly sliced

1/2 teaspoon salt

Several grinds black pepper, to
   taste

6 butter lettuce leaves

This "BLT" (or perhaps it should be called a "TLT") features grilled tofu that is smoked with wood chips as it grills. It will become one of your favorites.

Preheat the grill to high with a smoker box in place. Cut the slab of tofu through the middle to create 2 pieces. Place each piece on a paper towel and cover with another towel. Place a heavy skillet on top to press the excess water from the tofu. After 15 minutes, place the slabs between fresh towels and repeat the process. Cut the tofu into 12 thin slices. Brush each side of tofu with the sesame oil and place the slices on the grill. Grill for 6 to 7 minutes, turn, and grill for 6 to 7 more minutes.

Evenly coat one side of each slice of bread with the butter. Place the bread, buttered sides down, on the grill and grill for about 2 minutes, until the bread is toasted and shows grill marks. Place the bread on a work surface, grilled sides down. Coat half of the slices with equal amounts of mayonnaise and the remaining slices with mustard. Place equal amounts of the grilled tofu on the mustard-coated slices. Top the tofu with the tomato, salt, and black pepper. Cover with lettuce leaves and the mayonnaise-coated slice of bread. Cut the sandwiches in half and serve immediately.

Yield: 6 main-dish servings

Grilled Cheese Sandwiches
with Cremini Mushrooms

INGREDIENTS

2 tablespoons (28 milliliters) olive oil

2 teaspoons crushed garlic

1 1/4 pounds (570 grams) cremini mushrooms

8 slices sourdough sandwich bread

2 tablespoons (30 grams) Dijon mustard

16 slices Provolone cheese (about 8 ounces/225 grams)

2 tablespoons (28 grams) unsalted butter, melted

Everyone loves grilled cheese sandwiches, but this version is a gourmet delight. Grilling the mushrooms and then placing them inside the sandwiches creates a wonderful flavor.

Preheat the grill to medium. Place the olive oil and garlic in a bowl and whisk together to combine. Place the mushrooms in a bag and drizzle the olive oil mixture over them. Twist the bag to seal, allowing some air to remain in the bag. Toss gently to coat the mushrooms evenly. Place the mushrooms on the grill stem side up and grill for about 5 minutes. Turn and continue to grill for about 5 minutes. Remove the mushrooms from the grill and set aside. Slice the mushrooms when cool enough to handle.

Meanwhile, spread one side of each slice of bread with a thin layer of mustard. Evenly layer each slice with the Provolone cheese and then place equal amounts of the mushroom slices on one side of the bread, then top with the other slice of the bread. Use a pastry brush to lightly coat the outer sides of the bread with the butter. Place the sandwiches on the grill and grill for 4 to 5 minutes, turn, and grill for 3 to 4 more minutes. Slice the sandwiches in half and serve immediately.

Yield: 4 main-dish servings

Grilled Tempeh Burgers

INGREDIENTS

2 packages soy tempeh (8 ounces/225 grams each)

1/4 cup (60 milliliters) soy sauce

2 tablespoons (28 milliliters) canola oil

2 tablespoons (28 milliliters) dark sesame oil

4 teaspoons crushed garlic

6 sesame-seed buns

I large tomato, sliced

6 butter lettuce leaves

Serve this burger with your favorite condiments, such as mayonnaise, mustard, ketchup, and pickles. It has a hearty, meaty texture and flavor.

Carefully slice each piece of tempeh to create 6 thin slices.

In a small bowl, whisk together the soy sauce, canola oil, sesame oil, and garlic. Pour the mixture into a lipped baking sheet and place the tempeh on top. Marinate the tempeh for about 30 minutes, carefully turning several times.

Preheat the grill to medium. Place the tempeh on the grill and grill for 3 to 4 minutes. Carefully turn the tempeh and continue to grill for 3 to 4 more minutes.

Meanwhile, slice the sesame-seed buns in half and place them, cut sides down, on the grill to toast for a few minutes.

To serve, place the tempeh on one side of each bun. Allow each diner to garnish as desired with the tomato and lettuce.

Yield: 6 main-dish servings

Tofu Burgers

Serve these classic vegetarian burgers with pickles, mustard or ketchup, and mayonnaise.

INGREDIENTS

- $\frac{1}{2}$ cup (100 grams) uncooked sushi rice
- 14 ounces (400 grams) firm tofu
- $\frac{1}{3}$ cup (35 grams) bread crumbs
- $\frac{1}{2}$ cup (80 grams) diced white onion
- 1 tablespoon (14 milliliters) olive oil
- 1 tablespoon (14 milliliters) soy sauce
- 1 teaspoons crushed garlic
- 1 teaspoon vegetarian-style Worcestershire sauce
- Dash liquid smoke
- 1 egg, beaten
- 2 tablespoons (28 milliliters) canola oil
- 8 whole wheat buns
- 2 large tomatoes, sliced
- $\frac{1}{2}$ hcad iceberg lettuce, shredded

Bring $1\frac{1}{4}$ cups (300 milliliters) water to a boil on the stovetop in a saucepan, then stir in the rice. Cover, reduce the heat to very low, and cook for about 20 minutes, until the water is absorbed. Remove the saucepan from the heat and set aside, covered, for about 5 minutes.

Meanwhile, cut the tofu into $\frac{1}{2}$-inch slices and place them on a paper towel. Cover with another towel and gently press to remove as much of the moisture as possible. Crumble the tofu into a bowl. Stir in the bread crumbs, onion, olive oil, soy sauce, garlic, Worcestershire sauce, liquid smoke, and egg. Add the rice and stir to combine. Use your hands to form into 8 patties. Set them aside on a platter.

Preheat the grill to high. Place 2 fajita pans or a cast-iron skillet on the grill to heat. Coat with the canola oil and place the patties on to cook. Cook for about 8 minutes, turn, and continue to cook for another 8 minutes, until heated through.

Slice the buns in half and place them, cut sides down, on the grill to toast for a few minutes.

To serve, place the patties on one side of each bun. Allow each diner to garnish as desired with the tomatoes and lettuce.

Yield: 8 main-dish servings

CHAPTER 11
Grilled Desserts

The perfect way to end a grilled meal is with a flavorful grilled fruit dessert. The grill will still be hot enough, or it may quickly be reheated, to sear some fresh fruit to enjoy in a variety of ways. Always choose firm, ripe fruit so that it will stand up to the grill temperature.

Grilled desserts are quick to prepare and to take from the grill to the table, so consider them even when you are not preparing a grilled meal. Fruit from the grill is a delicious way to get one of those recommended fruit servings into your daily diet!

Most of these grilled desserts are seasonal, so you will want to enjoy the particular fruit when it is at its peak. Strawberries and cherries are a sign that spring is finally here. Serve the Strawberries Soaked in Late-Harvest Riesling (page 206) with grilled pound cake for an interesting twist to the traditional strawberry shortcake. Grilled Bing and Queen Anne Cherries (page 207) will make you yearn for the first cherries of the season, as grilling the cherries unlocks the natural sugars and sparks the flavor.

As the season progresses, new fruits become the stars. When apricots appear, be sure to serve Grilled Apricots with Chocolate Mousse (page 207), a guaranteed palate-pleaser. Peaches ripen next, along with nectarines. Choose cling-free varieties to cut in half and place on the grill. Yellow Peaches with Ginger Glaze (page 209) is sure to delight family and friends. Pears and cantaloupe are mid- to late-summer fruits. Enjoy Grilled Red Bartlett Pears with Savory Ricotta Cheese (page 208) and Cantaloupe with Frozen Yogurt (page 211) with your summertime meals.

Tropical bananas and pineapples are always available, so anytime you want to fire up the grill, consider Grilled Pineapple with Balsamic Vinegar and Brown Sugar (page 213) or Grilled Bananas with Ice Cream and Chocolate (page 210). They will bring that spark of summer to the winter table.

Prepared pound cake may also be placed on the grill just long enough to develop grill marks for an interesting presentation as an accompaniment to most grilled fruits. Feel free to substitute frozen yogurt or tofu ice cream in the recipes that call for ice cream. Have fun with the recipes in this chapter and use them to inspire your own creations.

Strawberries
Soaked in Late-Harvest Riesling

INGREDIENTS

8 large strawberries, hulled

1 cup (235 milliliters) late-harvest Riesling

1/2 cup (120 milliliters) whipping cream

1 tablespoon (12 grams) sugar

1/4 teaspoon vanilla

This is a simple but lovely way to end a spring or early summer meal. Choose the largest strawberries that you can. Purchase a pound cake and place slices on the grill to serve with the strawberries.

Place the strawberries in a bowl. Pour the Riesling over them and allow them to soak for about 20 minutes.

Put the whipping cream in a cold bowl and whip until soft peaks begin to form. Add the sugar and vanilla and whip to incorporate. Place in the refrigerator until needed.

When you are ready to serve, preheat the grill to medium. Place the whole strawberries on the grill. Cook for 6 to 8 minutes, turning frequently. Spoon equal portions of the whipped cream into 4 small bowls. Place 2 strawberries in each bowl and serve immediately.

Yield: 4 servings

Grilled Apricots
with Chocolate Mousse

My niece, Natalie Geiskopf, loves to create desserts. She developed this mousse recipe, which is embellished with grilled apricots. Serve with a glass of port, if you wish.

INGREDIENTS

1¼ pounds (570 grams) silken tofu

3 tablespoons (45 milliliters) milk

2 tablespoons (25 grams) sugar

¾ cup (170 grams) semi-sweet chocolate chips

6 large apricots

Place the tofu in a blender or food processor and add the milk and sugar. Puree until smooth.

Melt the chocolate chips in a double boiler or microwave oven. Add to the tofu mixture and puree to incorporate. Spoon the mousse into small dessert dishes and place in the refrigerator for several hours to chill.

Preheat the grill to medium-high. Cut the apricots in half and place them cut sides down on the grill. Cover the grill and grill for 5 to 7 minutes until soft. Arrange 2 halves on top of each of the 6 mousse servings.

Yield: 6 servings

Grilled Bing and
Queen Anne Cherries

Grilling cherries may not be the first thought that comes to mind, but once you have tried this dessert, you will be looking forward to cherry season every year! You may use all Bing cherries if the Queen Anne variety is not available.

INGREDIENTS

½ pound (225 grams) firm Bing cherries

½ pound (225 grams) firm Queen Anne cherries

1 cup (235 milliliters) late-harvest dessert wine

6 scoops chocolate ice cream

Stem the cherries and place them in a bowl. Pour the dessert wine over them and allow them to soak for about 15 minutes.

When you are ready to serve, preheat the grill to medium. Most grill racks are designed so that the cherries will not fall through the slats. If yours has wide openings, place the cherries in a grill basket or mesh rack. Grill for about 3 minutes, until the cherries burst. Place one scoop of ice cream on 6 individual plates and top with the cherries.

Yield: 6 servings

Nectarines
with Almond Glaze

Choose a freestone nectarine for this flavorful dessert. I like the flavor of Torani Syrup, but you may use a different variety of almond-flavored syrup or even amaretto.

INGREDIENTS

2 tablespoons (28 milliliters) almond syrup

2 tablespoons (40 grams) honey

2 tablespoons (28 grams) unsalted butter, melted

4 firm, ripe nectarines

8 scoops ice cream

Place the almond syrup, honey, and butter in a small bowl and mix to combine. Set aside.

When you are ready to serve, preheat the grill to medium. Cut the nectarines in half and remove the pits. Brush some of the almond mixture on the cut sides of the nectarines, then place the nectarines cut sides down on the grill. Reserve the rest of the almond mixture. Grill the nectarines for 5 to 8 minutes, until the juices begin to drip and the nectarines are slightly soft.

Place the grilled nectarine halves on 8 individual serving plates with a scoop of ice cream. Drizzle with the remaining almond mixture and serve.

Yield: 8 servings

Grilled Red Bartlett Pears
with Savory Ricotta Cheese

INGREDIENTS

7 1/2 ounces (210 grams) ricotta cheese

1/8 teaspoon cinnamon

Several grinds nutmeg, to taste

2 firm, ripe Bartlett pears

1 tablespoon (14 grams) unsalted butter, melted

2 tablespoons (40 grams) honey, warmed

4 sprigs fresh mint

Most Bartlett pears are the popular green-skinned types that turn golden yellow when ripe. Growers have developed a red-skinned variety that is particularly pretty—seek them out at your local farmers' market. Either variety is delicious when prepared for this dessert. Make sure the pears are firm but ripe, not too soft.

Place the ricotta cheese in a bowl and stir in the cinnamon and nutmeg. Set aside in the refrigerator until needed.

When you are ready to serve, preheat the grill to medium. Cut the pears in half lengthwise and remove and discard the cores, leaving the halves intact. Use a pastry brush to coat the cut sides with the melted butter. Transfer the pears to the grill, cut sides down. Grill for about 4 minutes.

Place equal amounts of the ricotta cheese mixture on 4 individual serving plates. Top each with a pear half. Drizzle with the honey and garnish with the mint sprigs.

Yield: 4 servings

Yellow Peaches
with Ginger Glaze

Freestone peaches are the best choice for this easy and elegant dessert. Choose firm yellow peaches—not ones that are ready-to-eat ripe.

INGREDIENTS

3 teaspoons grated fresh ginger, firmly packed

3/4 cup (255 grams) honey

4 firm, ripe peaches

8 scoops vanilla ice cream

Fresh mint sprigs

Place 1/2 cup (120 milliliters) water in a small saucepan on the stovetop and add the ginger. Bring to a rapid simmer over medium-high heat. Add the honey and continue to cook until reduced by half, stirring occasionally. Remove the saucepan from the heat and set aside to cool. Strain to remove the ginger.

When you are ready to serve, preheat the grill to medium. Cut the peaches in half and remove the pits. Brush some of the ginger mixture on the cut sides of the peaches, then place the peaches cut sides down on the grill. Grill for 5 to 8 minutes, until juices begin to drip and the peaches are slightly soft.

Meanwhile, put the remaining ginger mixture in a small saucepan and place on the stovetop over medium heat. Cook to caramelize, stirring frequently. Place the grilled peach halves on 8 individual serving plates with a scoop of ice cream. Drizzle with the ginger sauce and garnish with the mint.

Yield: 8 servings

Grilled Bananas
with Ice Cream and Chocolate

4 firm, ripe bananas or
   8 Manzano bananas

I tablespoon (14 grams)
   unsalted butter, melted

I tablespoon (14 milliliters)
   apricot brandy

I tablespoon (20 grams) honey

Pinch cinnamon

Several grinds nutmeg, to taste

8 small scoops vanilla ice cream

$1/2$ cup (120 milliliters)
   chocolate syrup

12 fresh cherries (optional)

There are many varieties of bananas in addition to the Cavendish variety that you typically find at the supermarket. If you can find the Manzano—also called finger bananas—use them, as they are especially attractive for this dish.

When you are ready to serve, preheat the grill to medium. Peel the bananas and cut in half lengthwise.

In a saucepan, melt the butter and add the apricot brandy, honey, cinnamon, and nutmeg. Brush the bananas with the butter mixture and place them crosswise on the grill or on a grilling grate. Grill for about 4 minutes, turning once.

To serve, arrange the bananas in 4 shallow dishes and top with 2 scoops of ice cream. Drizzle with the chocolate sauce. Top with the cherries, if desired.

Yield: 4 servings

Cantaloupe with Frozen Yogurt

INGREDIENTS

1/2 ripe cantaloupe

4 scoops frozen vanilla yogurt

4 tablespoons Fresh Blueberry
Sauce (page 33)

4 sprigs fresh mint

Cantaloupe is always good icy cold, but this grilled version brings out the natural sugars of the melon and is delicious with frozen yogurt.

When you are ready to serve, preheat the grill to medium. Without peeling, cut the cantaloupe into 8 slices. Place the cantaloupe on the grill and grill for 2 to 3 minutes on each side. Remove from the grill and place 2 slices on each of the 4 serving plates. Top each serving of cantaloupe with a scoop of frozen yogurt and a drizzle of Fresh Blueberry Sauce. Garnish with the mint.

Yield: 4 servings

Bartlett Pears
with Butterscotch Sauce

Choose firm, ripe pears for this dessert. Make the sauce ahead of time to allow it to cool. Garnish with mint sprigs and serve with cookies.

INGREDIENTS

1/3 cup (75 grams) packed
   brown sugar

1/4 cup (60 milliliters) light
   corn syrup

2 tablespoons (28 grams)
   unsalted butter

1/4 cup (60 milliliters)
   whipping cream

1/2 teaspoon vanilla extract

Several grinds fresh nutmeg,
   to taste

2 firm, ripe Bartlett pears

Mint sprigs

Place the brown sugar, corn syrup, and 1 tablespoon of the butter in a small saucepan on the stovetop. Bring to a boil over medium heat, stirring constantly. Boil for about 1 minute and remove from the heat. Stir in the cream, vanilla, and nutmeg. Cool for at least 30 minutes before serving. (The sauce will thicken as it cools. You may refrigerate it, but bring it to room temperature before serving.)

When you are ready to serve, preheat the grill to medium. Cut the pears in half lengthwise and remove and discard the cores, leaving the halves intact. Melt the remaining 1 tablespoon of butter and use a pastry brush to coat the cut sides of the pears. Transfer the pears to the grill, cut sides down. Grill for about 4 minutes. Remove the pears from the grill and place on 4 individual serving plates. Drizzle with the butterscotch sauce and serve immediately. Garnish with the mint.

Yield: 4 servings

Grilled Plantains with
Chocolate Sauce and Almonds

INGREDIENTS

I plantain

I tablespoon (14 grams) unsalted
    butter, melted

4 scoops vanilla ice cream

Chocolate syrup

2 tablespoons (15 grams) chopped
    dry-roasted almonds

Plantains are large green-skinned fruit that look like bananas. This member of the banana family has a more starchy texture than the common yellow Cavendish banana. It is best when cooked before serving. Try a caramel sauce or Fresh Blueberry Sauce (page 33) for a variation.

When you are ready to serve, preheat the grill to medium. Remove and discard the stem end of the plantain and, without peeling it, cut into 4 equal pieces. Brush the cut sides with butter and place on the grill. Grill for 5 to 6 minutes, turning several times. (The plantain will begin to caramelize, and you will smell the sweetness.) Remove the plantain from the grill and peel off the skin. Cut each piece in half lengthwise and place 2 halves on 4 individual serving plates. Put a scoop of ice cream on each plate and drizzle with chocolate syrup. Top with equal an amount of the almonds and serve immediately.

Yield: 4 servings

Grilled Pineapple with
Balsamic Vinegar and Brown Sugar

INGREDIENTS

1 ripe golden pineapple

3 tablespoons (45 grams)
   unsalted butter, melted

1/4 cup (60 milliliters) balsamic
   vinegar

1/4 cup (75 grams) brown sugar

This is a very simple, but simply delicious, dessert. To select a ripe pineapple, look for a golden tone to the skin. Pull one of the center leaves from the top of the pineapple. If it releases easily, the pineapple is perfectly ripe.

Place the pineapple on its side on a cutting board and cut off the top with the leaves (reserve to garnish the serving platter, if desired) and the bottom end. Set the pineapple upright and cut the rind from the fruit in lengthwise strips, slicing deep enough to remove the eyes. Cut the pineapple in half crosswise into 1/2-inch thick slices. Remove the fibrous core from the center of each slice using a sharp knife or a melon baller.

When you are ready to serve, preheat the grill to medium. Brush both sides of the pineapple slices with the melted butter and place on the grill. Grill for 4 to 6 minutes, turn, and continue to grill for about 4 minutes. Drizzle equal amounts of the balsamic vinegar over each slice and top with equal amounts of brown sugar. Continue to grill for 1 to 2 minutes. (The sugar will melt into the pineapple, and both sides will have grill marks.) Place pineapple slices on a platter with the reserved pineapple leaves in the center or place slices on individual serving plates. Serve immediately.

Yield: 6 servings

Glossary of Specialty Ingredients

Arborio rice. This short, oval-shaped rice is the key ingredient necessary to produce the classic, creamy rice preparation called risotto. Risotto is the signature comfort-food dish of Northern Italy. Shop for Arborio rice in Italian markets and natural food stores.

Asiago. Asiago is usually sold as an aged, dried cheese that comes in a block or grated form. It is less salty than Parmesan and has its own unique nutty flavor.

Balsamic vinegar. This vinegar is uniquely rich, with a dense yet mellow flavor. True balsamic vinegar is produced in the Italian province of Modena according to ancient techniques. It is aged for ten to fifty years in wooden barrels before bottling.

Basmati rice. This aromatic rice is primarily grown in India and Pakistan. It is available in white and brown varieties. Briefly rinse the rice before cooking for a light and fluffy texture.

Bok choy. Also called Chinese cabbage, this vegetable is used extensively in Asian cooking. The dark-green leaves are attached to thick, smooth white stems. The leaves have a slightly peppery taste; the stems are somewhat sweeter and quite succulent. Shop for baby bok choy at farmers' markets.

Broccoli rabe. Known as *cime di rapa* or *rapini* in Italy, this wild form of broccoli is prized for its sharp, bitter flavor. It resembles a very thin, leafy broccoli stalk with no pronounced head. Shop for it in Italian markets and local farmers' markets from fall through early spring.

Bulgur wheat. Bulgur is produced from whole wheat kernels. The kernels are steam-cooked, then dried and cracked into a coarse, medium, or fine grain.

Cannellini beans. These white, kidney-shaped beans have a mildly nutty flavor and hail from Tuscany. These beans may be purchased dried or canned at Italian groceries or natural food stores.

Chapati. This Indian flat bread looks much like a flour tortilla but is made from whole wheat flour. Use it as you would use a flour tortilla for a more nutritious wrap.

Chipotle chiles in adobo. These are smoked jalapeños that are canned *en adobo*—in a rich sauce made from tomatoes, vinegar, and spices. They have a distinctive, smoky flavor and are quite hot, so a little goes a long way. Shop for them in Mexican markets and well-stocked groceries.

Couscous. This semolina pasta traces its roots to northern Africa. It is made from precooked semolina wheat, and the resulting tiny grains of couscous cook quickly when added to a small amount of boiling water.

Crema. This slightly soured cream is often served in Mexico as a table condiment. It is neither as sour nor as thick as standard supermarket sour cream. Shop for it in Mexican markets and well-stocked grocery stores.

Crème fraîche. This slightly soured cream has a semi-thick texture—but not as thick as standard sour cream—with a tart, piquant flavor. It is used extensively in Mediterranean, French, and Italian cooking. Shop for it in Italian markets or in specialty grocery stores.

Crostini. Crostini is an Italian word that refers to crunchy grilled or oven-baked toasts made from slightly stale bread. Crostini is most frequently eaten with a variety of savory toppings.

Dried tomatoes. Also referred to as sun-dried tomatoes, they have an intense flavor and a chewy texture. They are sold dried or reconstituted in olive oil. Most recipes call for the dried variety. They should be reconstituted before using in a recipe. To reconstitute sun-dried tomatoes, place them in a small bowl and cover them with water to soak for about 30 minutes, or place the bowl in the microwave for about a minute. Squeeze out most of the liquid and chop as called for in the recipe.

Endive. Also known as Belgian endive or witloof chicory, this smooth, pale, elongated vegetable is comprised of tightly closed, creamy yellow or white leaves. The flavor is slightly bitter, and the texture is both crisp and velvety.

Fermented black beans. The fermentation of these black beans (also called turtle beans) causes them to be quite salty. They are popular in Japanese and Chinese cooking, and it is best to rinse them before using. Look for them in Asian specialty markets and natural food stores.

Garlic. Garlic is sold in many forms, including fresh, crushed, and granulated. Each adds a pungent punch. Fresh garlic is sold in bulbs and is baked whole to produce a paste or separated into individual cloves, peeled, and then sliced, chopped, or minced before using. Crushed garlic comes in a jar and is ready to add to a recipe in a measured amount. Granulated garlic is a dried form with a texture similar to that of coarse salt.

Jícama. Jícama has a sweet, white flesh that maintains its delectable crispness for a long time after it is cut. It is a root vegetable that has a light brown skin that is stringy and should always be stripped off before using.

Kalamata olives. Sometimes called calamata olives, these succulent purple-black olives are native to Greece. They have an intense and piquant flavor.

Lemon grass. There is no substitute for the flavor of fresh lemon grass. The outer green is stripped away from the thick grass stalk to reveal a white center. This is finely minced or crushed before being added to a recipe. You can buy plants from herb farms and catalogs, and they're easy to grow in pots. Or shop for the stalks at an Asian market.

Mirin. Mirin is the sweet counterpart to sake, the Japanese rice wine. It is used extensively in Asian cooking, adding an interesting flavor note to many recipes.

Miso. Miso is a fermented soybean paste. Some varieties are intensely salty, while others have a mellow, sweeter flavor. Mild, light-colored miso is less salty than the darker varieties; shop for it at Asian markets or natural food stores.

Nopales. Also called nopalitos, these paddles are harvested from the prickly pear cacti that grow prolifically in central Mexico and some parts of the Southwestern United States. They have a succulent texture and a distinctive fresh flavor with just a hint of tartness. Nopales are sold fresh year-round in most Mexican markets. Canned nopalitos are also available, but the texture and flavor is not as good as that of fresh nopalitos.

Parchment paper. Sometimes referred to as cooking or baking parchment, this heat-proof paper is used for *en papillote* cooking—the classic French meal-in-a-pouch preparation. Shop for it in grocery stores, usually displayed with the other standard kitchen wraps.

Pickled jalapeños. The pickling process adds a pleasant, piquant note to this hot pepper, which is sold in jars and is readily available year-round. Shop for them in Mexican markets or well-stocked grocery stores.

Polenta. Polenta is dried corn ground into a medium-grain meal. Italian markets and natural food stores sell it labeled "polenta," but fine-ground American cornmeal can be substituted if you can't find polenta itself.

Ponzu sauce. This is a citrus-seasoned soy sauce that is delightful as a table condiment and adds a unique flavor note when used as an ingredient in a recipe. Shop for it in Asian markets.

Portobello mushrooms. These large mushrooms can measure 4 to 6 inches across. They have a good, solid, "meaty" texture. They are widely available in grocery stores and in Italian and specialty markets.

Queso fresco. This part-skim cheese has a mild flavor and a crumbly texture. It is used primarily as a topping rather than a filling, since it does not melt smoothly. Shop for it in Mexican markets or well-stocked grocery stores.

Radicchio. The most common variety of this vegetable is purple, mottled with white. The small heads have a bitter flavor note, and they are sold in the produce section of specialty grocery stores or at farmers' markets.

Rice wine vinegar. This vinegar has a sweet yet tart flavor, and it is delicious sprinkled over raw vegetables or used as an ingredient in many sauces and salad dressings.

Sesame tahini. Tahini is ground raw or toasted sesame seeds. The resulting spread has a texture similar to smooth peanut butter. Shop for it at Asian markets or natural food stores.

Shiitake mushrooms. These mushrooms are available fresh or dried in Asian markets and some grocery stores. They have a rich flavor and chewy texture, so it's best to slice or chop them before using. The dried variety needs to be reconstituted before using. To reconstitute, place them in a small bowl and cover them with water to soak for about 30 minutes, or place the bowl in the microwave for about a minute. Squeeze out most of the liquid and chop as called for in the recipe.

Soba. Soba is a thin Japanese noodle typically made with buckwheat flour. For the best selection, shop for them at an Asian market.

Sweet chili sauce. This prepared, sweet, hot chili sauce adds a distinctive flavor when used as an ingredient in a recipe or served as a table condiment. Shop for it at Asian markets.

Tempeh. Tempeh is produced by fermenting whole soybeans, sometimes combining them with other grains. This high-protein food is very dense and has a chewy texture with a nutty flavor.

Tofu. Tofu is made from soy milk that has been coagulated to form curds. The blandness of this high-protein food makes it very versatile, as it readily takes on the flavors paired with it. Tofu comes in various textures, from soft and silky to dense and chewy. Each variety is suitable for different types of dishes. Shop for tofu at natural food stores, Asian markets, and most well-stocked grocery stores.

Tomatillos. Tomatillos grow inside paper husks, which is discarded before the cherry tomato–size tomatillos are cooked. They are firm in texture and lime green in color with a tart, fresh flavor that is essential to many traditional Mexican dishes. Shop for them in Mexican markets and well-stocked grocery stores. Canned tomatillos are also available and can be used when fresh ones aren't in season.

Wasabi. Wasabi, a pungent green form of Asian horseradish, is commonly sold in a dry form that is mixed with water or rice wine vinegar before using. Shop for it packaged in small tins at Asian markets or well-stocked grocery stores.

Index